Economics for BIG Kids

Subtitle: Free Enterprise and Capitalism for Beginners

(THE UN-ILLUSTRATED VERSION)

By   Carrington   B.   Davis

Copyright   Washington, DC 2013

TABLE OF CONTENTS

Contents

Preface 3

What is Economics? 6

How's it Work? 25

How'd It Start? 32

Kings to Constituents 43

What's Our Stake? 59

Banks are People, Too.. 72

Class Warfare 83

What's Free Enterprise? 98

America, the Beautiful 110

The Melting Pot 118

Give Us Your Tired 129

Measuring the Money... 139

The New World Order 156

What's The Way Out? 166

About the Author.. 182

Preface

Around the time of the election of 2012, I caught some information that popped up on television that I thought made a statement about today's economy. A news blurb talked about a list of the top five highest paid deceased personalities in this year's economy, those celebrities that have passed away who are generating revenues in 2012.

The list began with Bob Marley at $17 million. He was number five. Above him, at $39 million, was Charles Schultz, the creator of the Peanuts comic strip. Elvis Presley came in third at $55 million. Just above Elvis was Michael Jackson at $145 million. At the top of the list was Elizabeth Taylor. Her revenues for the year were $210 million. She has perfume and other products in the marketplace, but I do remember that they sold a lot of her jewelry from her estate this year.

These people demonstrate the new economy we live in, the Facebook, in-your-face, every man is a star economy that promotes the viability of each individual as an asset. This is the new age of global telecommunications. Every individual has the ability to reach the world. This allows each individual to potentially provide a unique perspective to every other individual. In this new world, my five-year-old nephew is just beginning to live in an economy that is emerging from decades, if not centuries of evolution. His success is going to depend on his knowledge of the economic system that he will inherit and his understanding and knowledge of the economic system from which it came.

My nephew is the hope of the world. When I had a recent conversation with his mother, I discovered a lot of what I knew about economics and a lot of what some of us do not know about the subject matter, from job creation to the role of government. I found that my niece was not much more informed about the subject of economics than her five-year-old son, and she had more than a college degree and almost two decades of professional life.

The purpose of this writing is to encourage people to understand the science and art of economics as a prelude to marketing themselves in a new world where money moves at the speed of light. People need to be aware of the mechanics of the economic system, especially since they have a role to play as economic policy makers in a democratic society. The election of 2012 demonstrated clearly that most people have little idea what economics is or how it works. Most people have no idea about the role of government or its economic impact. Most people have no idea how jobs are created or how that process can be influenced. This book is designed to help stimulate interest and guide people to a knowledge of economics, albeit at the level of a five-year-old. I hope you like it, and I hope your five-year-old gets a kick out of it too.

Carrington B. Davis

Washington, DC

What is Economics?

The day was bright and I was looking forward to a visit from my niece and her five-year-old son. As I sat on the porch and enjoyed the view, my mind wandered to a time when I was young. I thought about a moment in time when a man came by to visit my father. He was very well dressed in a nice suit and a long tweed overcoat. He was a bit stocky, but not fat. And he was a pleasant person to be around.

I remember this visit because my father told me his story after the man left. My father worked at the Bureau of Engraving and Printing in Washington DC where all the paper money is produced. This man and my father worked together. My father told me that one day this gentleman was late coming back from lunch because he sat in the park and drew pictures. I guess he became so engaged in his art that he lost track of time. In either case, he was fired for that. My father told me that he pursued his love of art and followed that dream to become, at that time, the Art Director for CBS Television in New York City.

This was very interesting to me, at that time, since this man was an African American and this happened in the 1950s. I was encouraged by this story because it reminded me that each and every individual has a potential to create their own destiny. My father used this experience to encourage me to study Art in college, which I did until I discovered I didn't want to be an Artist and changed my major concentration to Business Administration and Economics.

Sometimes events in your childhood teach you things that you do not remember until you are older and the world has changed. With my niece's son coming over, a five-year-old boy, I wondered what the world would be like when he grows up, knowing that he has no limits except his own imagination and an education in the economics of the planet.

In 30 years, it will be a new world. Not only will technology expand our ability to solve many of the problems we face today, but we will also have new problems resulting from the melting ice caps and the trash pile of plastic and garbage that is floating in the Pacific Ocean as a result of the Japanese tsunami of 2010.

The oceans are being overfished and the population of the earth will be close to 12 billion by that time, if not sooner. The mineral resources that we have will not last forever and global warming may change everything. And who knows what new economic innovations will create the future employment opportunities. All these things wandered through my mind as I watched the trees flow with the breeze in anticipation of the day's events. And lo and behold the screen door opened.

The great thing about a five-year-old kid is that they'll listen to you if it's something they're interested in. And sometimes, even if they don't know it, they remember these things for the rest of their lives. I can remember events as a child, events that stick out in my mind, even though I cannot remember much else about what happened. I remember the situation and the people, but I don't remember the significance. After we got settled, as I sat and spoke with my niece Melanie and her male child Bret on the enclosed porch of the house, I remembered the little day dream, vision memory I had about my father's friend. That was my memory.

As the day moved along, while discussing current events with my niece, she asked me some questions that led me to feel the importance of the conversation in the presence of her son. I began to notice that, while in the midst of play with his array of toys, he was focused on our every word. I had my laptop with me and would, from time to time, browse it for information to add to my conversation. At some point in the conversation, I sensed that our playmate was a "student of the moment". I thought of this as one of those times, like in my life, when you are around somebody that you will always remember, as if it were yesterday. So, I went with the spirit.

This was the year 2012. It was a time when people thought about the Mayan calendar and the end of the world as we know it, and all that jazz which obviously didn't happen. We started about that, Melanie and I, and we began talking about the current political situation, the upcoming election, and all of the issues surrounding globalization. We would laugh a bit here and there, since Melanie can't keep things too serious for too long. We talked about the issues of poverty and the financial crises that we faced as a country.

As the conversation evolved, some of the discussions and positions we saw in the Presidential Debate in the election season led us to discuss the economy. Economics, economics and more economics, with trickle-down theories and supply-side answers all around.

Government spending and tax cuts for the rich, welfare programs and entitlements, all these issues of government and private enterprise that arose during the campaign, we discussed them. We were discussing all these things and kept going on the web for answers, when we were interrupted by the third party on the porch.

"Ma, what is economics?" This was the soft shy inquiry of my five-year-old nephew as he twirled his plaything while listening to my niece and I discussing the ills of the world. He interrupted us as my niece Melanie was saying.

"So why can't someone tell me how to make this work.

"Make what work?", I retorted.

"This economy. How can we make this economy work? I've got this five-year-old to take care of and my grandmother as well. I can do a lot better, but the economy is just so bad."

These were the words of my niece Melanie as we sat on the porch on an autumn Sunday afternoon and chatted about this and that. This was the autumn of 2012 and the job market was as unsettled as the political season. Barack Obama was running for reelection, and of course, the economy was an issue. The Conservatives and the Republican Party were hell-bent on creating a picture of a President who did not understand the economy. The Ryan Budget and the Romney Plan were front and center, and the unemployment rate was heatedly debated, along with every financial statistic about the global marketplace. Disruptions in Europe and threats to the right to vote in America were in the atmosphere. So we were talking about economics.

I turned to Bret and asked him, "What were you saying?"

"What is economics?"

Melanie and I looked at each other with a questioning gaze. "Is he ready for this", we sort of said to ourselves.

Bret had heard us talking for some time after he followed us out onto the porch to keep us company with his toys in hand. He had made the rounds, saying hello to the throng of relatives and neighborhoods that were gathered to watch a Redskin game and celebrate a birthday. He was now with us.

Bret's an intelligent young man, inquisitive and articulate for his age. He was taught to read phonetically, growing up under the tutelage of his mother and his grandmother and his great-grandmother who is 93. He was homeschooled before he went to kindergarten. He wants to learn and is pretty good at it. Bret has his own way about things. He's a little spoiled, not that he wouldn't be since he is attractive, caring, entertaining and bit precocious, but he loves to learn and he will stop his play when there is something that lifts his brow. So when I began to talk to his mother about economics, he stopped what he was doing and twirled the toy in his hand as he listened intensely to our conversation.

He had been listening as the conversation evolved. Melanie and I talked about the election.

We talked about the issue of employment and the cost of taking care of an elderly person, and the education of the young people, and the impact of economic conditions on all of our lives. This brought us into a discussion about the election and the economics of it all. So after a glance between us, I turned to Bret to say what I have written in this book.

Melanie asked me what I thought about the idea of "job creators", something that seemed to permeate the political atmosphere during the election season of 2012. As I spoke, I had Bret in the corner of my mind and I told Melanie that the first thing a kid needs to know about economics is that everybody can participate. This has always been true because everybody has always had a say since they were a living, breathing, consuming, contributing person.

It's a human thing. Economics is the exchange of products, goods, and services through a meeting of supply and demand. This is called trade, and you can't have demand in the supply and demand system without people to demand things.

People use things or consume them. Without that, there is no need for an economy because there would be nobody to want stuff.

It's like playtime at school or working on a group project, everybody can participate.

"It's like being able to go to school or like watching television, everybody can participate and that's good. It hasn't always been that way, and it may not always be, but that what's up now". I said all this as I sipped a cup of tea and spoke with Melanie as she sat, ankles crossed and hands folded in her "professorial pose".

I told her, "We have to remember that there is no such thing as a job creator. It's not in the Dictionary (at least not yet). And if you can find one, please tell us who it is. Once you do, I'll go to that person and ask them to create all the jobs we need to have so that unemployment never exist again. As long as the magician, the Pied Piper of job creation is available, we will never have unemployment because the job creator will save us. There would no longer be any unemployment because the job creator will not allow that."

I went on to say, "Jobs are created by government. Jobs have always been created by government. From the time that people lived in a tribe, and no other form of government, the Chief would determine what the relationships in commerce were, in terms of buying and selling the harvest. The Chief would reconcile disputes. The Chief would establish exchanges between individuals. The Chief would do all the things that the President, the Congress, and the Federal Reserve does in our economy, as well as the banks and other institutions that oversee the quality and quantity of economic relationships."

In the modern era, and in the free enterprise system, if you don't want a bar brawl or a hockey fight, you need government. You cannot have a free enterprise system without regulation. We are lucky that the free enterprise system in this democracy allows us to work together to find solutions to problems. Political problems notwithstanding, everyone agrees when we all agree as to what works best for us all. –

The democracy. Without the democracy, there would be no free enterprise system.

That is because, without one man-one vote or full participation, you will have inefficiencies in the economic system that eventually will rise to the level of revolt when the people start saying "this thing ain't working'".

Government, any and every government, determines what is legitimate and what is illegal in trade. From the sale of slaves after the British outlawed the Slave Trade on the high seas to moonshiners who avoid taxation and dodge Revenuers during Prohibition (and to this day), to the drug prohibition laws, government makes rules about what can be included in commerce. During the period of Blue Laws, you couldn't sell alcohol on Sunday in Virginia, or most other Southern States.

The government determines the age of employment, outlawing child labor. The government sets standards for professionals and practitioners, and influencing the accreditations and certifications that are required in order to get a job.

Without government oversight, in any system, chaos prevails and nothing is more of a threat to economic activity than instability and anarchy. The free enterprise system requires government to set the rules and provide the referee.

Free enterprise is about the ability of the individual to be free of the impact of government on his or her ability to engage in commerce, and to create a level playing field, to control corruption and to resolve disputes. Freedom to engage in commerce is a freedom in America that comes from the freedoms in the Constitution, establishing individual freedom and Civil Rights. Civil Rights allow people to redress issues of the government and with those with whom they do business in State and Federal Court. Without the government, there is chaos. That's the role of government, to eliminate chaos and also to eliminate oppression. Everyone can play when the government protects individual rights from individuals and governments.

We live in interesting times. We live in a time of global economics.

Economics was not always global. It became global as the world became global. The discipline of Economics was created when a man named Adam Smith wrote a book about it in 1776. In this book, he spoke about four components of an economic system: land, labor, capital and entrepreneurship, with the entrepreneur being the guy who's in charge. He also talked about free markets, promoting the idea that the King (government) should allow freedom in trade between individuals without controls on trade and commerce from the King.

He also spoke of supply and demand as the determiner of prices, where people are free to negotiate and bargain between each other. In other words, he advocated freedom from the rules that served only the King, but served the individual as well, be he a laborer or an entrepreneur.

The way the economic system works depends on the time in history that we are talking about. Beginning with the Roman Empire, government was financed by an economy of Campaigns.

A Campaign was the practice of going to somebody else's territory and taking what you want. Thus, we have the Roman Empire. When Adam Smith wrote his book in 1776, the globalization of the world consisted of European colonialization of the Americas and a global trade expansion into India and China, with the exploitation of Africa from all sides.

But that was after the Roman Empire crumbled and a series of systems were set up to serve the interest of those in charge, at the expense of the majority who were not. These systems, serfdom, feudalism, and peasant farming gave power and control of the economy to Royalty, Aristocracy and the Ruling Class. This lasted for a period of time until global trade was so great that it required Royalty to release control of trade to Merchants. These Merchants would buy and sell the goods of the nations that the King's controlled. This time period was called Mercantilism, because the merchants filled the void for expanded trade and global efficiency until some other institutions for trade emerged.

The Kings ruled and governed until the new world, and the United States, created a form of Republican Democracy that allowed greater freedom for entrepreneurs and laborers. There was so much free land, land prices were low until the frontiers closed. Adam Smith advocated the free market system because it allowed for a natural balance between the owners and the workers in the negotiation of wages, and also created the natural price (rents) for land and the goods produced from it. All of this led people to other arguments about the government's role in establishing an economic system.

Karl Marx wrote a book that promoted a system call Communism which limited free enterprise and promoted the individual economic benefit of the workers through stable wages and work opportunities. Communism, Socialism or Democracy, they all determine the commercial and financial relationships within the society.

The American experience began as an English system. It evolved into a democratic system.

The economy, with the exception of the control of the cost of labor which incorporated the institution of slavery, allowed each person to be competitive. Or, at least all men, but we'll get to that momentarily.

In our historic past, we had a system of slavery. Slavery was an economic system that provided labor at controlled cost. An economy that can control costs is an economy that is stable and provides the opportunity to create surpluses that result from excesses generated by the control of cost. So the key to the free enterprise system is the ability of the people, through a government of full representation, to create economic stability so that free trade can take place.

In recent years there has been a rise in a group that calls themselves the Tea Party. They derive their name from the Boston Tea Party event in which men dressed as American Indians threw Tea into Boston Harbor to protest of the Stamp Act. This was prior to the Revolution and was one of the initial inspiring acts for it.

These people were protesting excessive taxation by Britain. At that time, Britain was engaged in a war, or had just finished a war, and needed to restore its coffers to pay off the war debt. I think it was the French and Indian War. So we got that Tea Tax.

The protest against taxes was fundamental. It was a protest of taxation without representation. In America today, the people have representation in the decisions about tax collection and the expenditures that the government makes with tax dollars. This right, the fact that we can vote in this democracy, means that the authority that taxes the people is subject to the will of the people. That means we are taxing ourselves. That is the goal of the United States of America, and it's Constitution which promotes a participatory economic philosophy, a "free" access to capital, land and the freedom to negotiate with labor. When there is representative government, the people determine the role of government and government's role in the economy. So the right to vote is economic power.

We the people, in order to form a more perfect union, have a democratic republic that allows us to create our own economic and fiscal policy. Fiscal policy is the decision of government to spend money. Monetary policy is the policy of controlling currencies through interest rates and the supply of money. When you get older, those of us who are still growing, you can look into John Maynard Keynes and the Monetarist and get a better understanding of what I'm talking about here.

Jobs and economic activity are created by government. This has been true since the monarchies. Adam Smith, the father of Economics, wrote about the power of the monarchy to control markets. This was in a time of colonialization around the world. In this colonialization, the government controlled the markets through grants, charters and Fiat. After all, it was all his or hers, wasn't it?

When capitalism was introduced, the idea was to encourage the monarchy to relinquish a degree of control over these markets and the allocation of assets.

This goes to the idea that, from the monarchy to democracy, economies have been created through the decisions and acts of government to establish laws that promote economic activity, rules to regulate commerce, even if those decisions are made of, for, and by the people. After all, if the King owned everything, the King got all the profits. So, where was the motivation for anyone to go forth and compete or conquer if he didn't keep some of the profits for himself?

How's it Work?

When I stopped, Melanie looked at me and nodded as if I should just keep going. I looked to Bret and he was just playing with a toy car, but he was all ears in my direction. So, I continued.

The Economy is affected by many things. The management of assets is one. The entrepreneur manages the land, the labor, and the capital. In the new age, they also manage "Information" as a product or service that has been created. Land was created by the Charter of the King to the colonial corporations who built America. Labor is created whenever there are sufficient people at the appropriate level to meet the demand for creating something out of the land or something out of what was created by the land. Capital is created by government as a regulated and acceptable, secured and stable legal tender medium of exchange to facilitate transactions in a capitalist system. We call this Currency.

Currency is something used as a "medium of exchange", like trading baseball cards for anything or having homemade cake in your school lunch. That cake can buy anything. Currency can also be created by an agreement among people to use sea shells or poker chips, since people have to agree to accept a common standard for it to work.

As an asset in this new age, we can see that Information has a value. Information is something that meets a demand for knowledge, understanding, or awareness to be valuable enough to the consumer to generate a price.

Whether that information is direct speech or a collection of music CDs, it is the information that is of value. Some information has a value unto itself because it assists in the operation of the capitalist system. It, therefore, has "intrinsic" value, and is said to be valuable in and of itself. Insider trader information is probably the prime example.

Any information that gives you an understanding of the economic situation and what is happening competitively or innovatively is of its own unique value to the capitalist system. If you see the Eddie Murphy movie, "Trading Places", you'll understand.

In order to solve any economic problem, you have to create more assets or you have to create a more efficient system. Sometimes you can do both. A more efficient system can be created by government when legislation refines and streamlines applications and requirements, such as for building permits that incorporate new technologies and energies.

An agreement to pass a law that regulates the transactions or activity in the economy is generally a solution. Examples are the various commissions created by the Congress to regulate interstate commerce, federal communications, banking, safety, health and labor relations are examples. This goes to the idea that, from the monarchy to democracy, economies have been created through the decisions of government to establish laws that promote economic activity.

"But, what about government regulations?" she asked. "I hear that's a problem." I went on.

Government regulations and enterprises help the economy expand. From the C&O canal, to the railroads across the nation, to Hoover Dam and the Tennessee Valley Authority, to the national defense highway system, to the regulation of the airways through the FCC and Banks through the Federal Reserve, government rules and interventions help.

The problem isn't government regulations, it's appropriate and effective regulations. As we saw with the financial crisis of 2008, and the ensuing global crisis in Europe, the ability of the government to agree on the appropriate and effective systems of governance and oversight is imperative to a growing productive economy, creating opportunity and hiring workers.
The ability to create economic activity is also a key. That ability relies on the ability to create new assets. So we notice that the entrepreneur has always worked with land, labor and capital.

We now recognize that the entrepreneur manages and oversees land, labor, capital, and information. So the key is to discover the way to enhance or increase or appreciate the value of land and the products that come from it. Or to organize or find new data or information that can be sold through electronic technologies, even if it's just a new music video of an old song.

Controlling the cost of labor is important, but since slavery was abolished in the United States and unionization has been permitted by law, the control of the cost of labor is outside the boundaries of the entrepreneur. Land is a limited resource, although the resources in and under the land are not limited, at least not in the same way. Whether it's growing more crops or discovering more oil, technology has allowed us to continually increase the productivity and value of land. New discoveries of how to use the land for highest and best use have also enhanced the value of the land.

Capital can be increased as well. The printing of money or the creation of financial instruments, such as credit default swaps and penny stocks, has led to an increase in capital.

Capital is, in many ways, a legal and binding promise to pay someone at a fixed time and fixed amount. It's a guarantee, just like the guarantee we see on the dollar bill which is signed by the Treasury Secretary, guaranteeing the "full faith and credit of the United States". Again, the role of government in maintaining the efficiency of these institutions is the key to increasing the value and availability of capital. When the government doesn't work, these assets of capital don't either. So we see that with effective government, the system works and capital increases. So if none of this is working, maybe the problem is we're not developing the right assets.

So what are the right assets in today's world, this new age? This is the information age, you know. The atomic age is over, the computer age is over, the age of flight, the jet age, and the satellite age are also over. In the information age, we have the ability to meet the challenges that we have faced throughout human history by incorporating all the lessons we have learned from the "Ages".

That challenge is to be creative, to go forth and multiply, and to create heaven on earth. This we can do because we have the ability to create new information out of the knowledge and wisdom of our minds and exchange it efficiently and effectively, one to another, at the speed of light.

Thanks to the Gutenberg press, we began this process whereby every man can receive his or her individual information needs in a book or technology that informs and educates instantly, globally. And this asset can be created every time each and every individual opens his or her mouth or sets to type, his or her ideas. The information becomes an asset because it can be exchanged. Each and every individual can become an Entrepreneur in today's world. We see this in 14 year old computer geeks and Internet game designers who have become millionaires through the distribution of their own knowledge. If they can do it, so can we all.

How'd It Start?

As I told Melanie, knowing that Bret was listening: The first name to know is the name Adam Smith. Adam Smith was a Scottish philosopher and writer who wrote a book that was published in 1776, the same year as the signing of the Declaration of Independence in the United States. We'll talk more about Adam Smith later, but the important thing to remember is that his book, his "Inquiry into the Nature and Causes of the Wealth of Nations", is the beginning of Economics.

Before Adam Smith, the term "Economics" was not used. The term "Capitalism" was not in use as well. Feudalism was the economic social and cultural order of the day and the feudal system was firmly entrenched, leaving very little mobility for the poor, the laborer or the farmer. It was a world where the King and the Royal Court ruled and the people struggled."

According to Adam Smith, there are four components of the economic system. They consist of land, labor, capital and entrepreneurship. Entrepreneurship is the management, oversight and motivation of the assets, the hard assets, of the earth.

When Adam Smith first wrote his essays, the field was known as the study of the Political Economy and was designed to give some understanding of a world in which colonialization and extended wealth was being impacted by the struggle for labor participation in the decisions about the cost of things, and the price of goods, and the compensation they should receive for the work they do. As Adam Smith wrote:

"The colony (that) a civilized nation, which takes possession either of a waste country, or of one so thinly inhabited that the natives easily give place to the new settlers, advances more rapidly to wealth and greatness than any other human society.

The colonialists carry out with them a knowledge (or know-how) of agriculture and of other useful arts superior to what can grow up of its own accord in the course of many centuries among savage and barbaric as nations.

They carry out with them, too, the habit of subordination, some notion of the regular government which takes place in their own country, and of the system of laws which supports it, and of a regular administration of justice; and they naturally establish something of the same kind in the new settlement."

I might add that Adam Smith's statement about the fast-track to wealth is similar in theory to the Roman Empire, in that, it is easiest to conquer than to develop. And this is true because primitive people are generally people who have not been prompted by circumstance, of God or man (other invaders), to invent or innovate. As Thomas Jefferson says, "Eternal vigilance is the price of freedom". And he might add that the people's investment in innovations and technology applications is the cost.

Adam Smith also wrote about concepts such as the division of labor, a concept of separating the work between people of various levels and uniqueness of skills so as to bring together a product through cooperation from the beginning to the end of the assembly or manufacturing process.

He spoke about the Principles which give cause or occasion to the division of labor and that the division of labor is limited by the extent of the market. He wrote about the origin of money and the idea that before coinage, people had to weigh or assay every time a transaction took place or risk counterfeit or under assessed values. His idea is that the cost and price of commodities is commensurate with the price of labor that it requires to obtain that commodity or to produce that product. He wrote, "Labor is the real exchange for commodities". And he took a position on the welfare of the Common Man. The Common Man is Joe Six-Pack, the average working man in the society, any society.

Adam Smith wrote about the Common Man in contrast to the Aristocrat or Entrepreneur, since you had to have money to get money in those days, inherited or granted.

He said, of the division of stock and of the nature, accumulation, and employment of stock, the following: "when the stock which a man possesses is no more than sufficient to maintain him for a few days or a few weeks, he seldom thinks of the rising any revenue from it.

He consumes it as daringly as he can, and endeavors by his labor to acquire something which may supply its place before it be consumed altogether. His revenue is, in this case, derived from his labor only. This is the state of the greater part of the laboring poor in all countries."

"But when he possesses stock sufficient to maintain him for months or years, he naturally endeavors to derive revenue from the greater part of it; reserving only so much for his immediate consumption as may maintain him till his revenue begins to come in. His whole stock, therefore, is just getting pushed into two parts. That part which, he expects, is to afford him this revenue, is called his capital."

So we see that Capital comes from having enough to not have to consume all that you have. This is called excess and excess is Capital. That was the question Adam smith hoped to address: What do we do with all this excess created by the discovery of the New World and the surplus created by control of the land through grants and labor though slavery?

Adam Smith saw money coming from rents, interests and profits as the source of capital accumulation. He also believed that the labor that adds to the value of the subject upon which it is bestowed is productive labor and that some labor, particularly menial labor, such as servants, "adds to the value of nothing".

Smith was critical of the current notion of Associations and Leagues such as the Chamber of Commerce and Industry groups when he took a position, vis-à-vis the relationship between workers and managers among themselves, the latter being the owners of capital, when he wrote the following:

"We rarely hear, it has been said, of the combinations of Masters, though frequently of those of workmen. But whoever imagines, upon this account that Masters rarely combine, is as ignorant of the world as the subject. Masters are always and everywhere in a sort of tacit, but constant and uniform, combination, not to raise the wages of labor above their actual rate. Masters to, sometimes enter into particular combinations to sink the wages of labor even below this rate.

These are always conducted with the utmost silence and secrecy till the moment of execution: and when the workmen yield, as they sometimes do without resistance, though severely felt by them, they are never heard of by other people."

He is saying further that when workers combine, "the Masters… never ceased to call allowed for the assistance of the civil magistrate, and the rigorous execution of those laws which have been enacted with so much severity against the combination of servants, laborers, and journeyman."

This tells us that, in Adam Smith's day, unions were taboo, and that combinations were forbidden by "laws which have been enacted". But unions happened in the US, nonetheless. That's democracy for you.

He speaks also to the idea of self motivation as the force that creates market competition and opportunity. This self interest is paramount to the idea of Capitalism, but Adam Smith often criticized actions that were based purely out of self interest and greed. He was an advocate of "Hands-Off" policies, sometimes called "Laissey-Faire" in French, which was the idea that the Monarchy should promote "free enterprise and exchange" without being required to be accountable to the Monarchy in private transactions and trade, as the role of government in the economic arena.

He also writes, "For ourselves, and nothing for other people, seems, in every age of the world, to have been the vile maxim of the Masters of mankind." All of this reflects Adam Smith's position on the struggle between the Royal class, or the Aristocracy, and the serfs, servants, laborers, workers, and peasants in Europe who are referred to as the Common Man in America.

His position suggests that the Common Man was at the mercy of the Aristocrats, with only pleas for justice as his hope. As we saw, the French Revolution of 1789 was another answer.

So, where does that lead us?", I asked. Melanie shrugged her shoulders and stared.

Throughout history, Entrepreneurs were responsible for overseeing these three hard assets, tangible assets of land, labor and capital. The asset that was missing is information, brought on by technology and the ability to sell that asset on books, CDs, and other physical devices., over the TV sets, the airwaves, the satellite, on the Internet, through IPhones and Smartphones, on Kindle and Notebooks.

It is not the devices that are the product, it's the information. In the Information Age, the ability to advise someone on the other side of the world, through the Internet, or to provide a physical presentation of information, has made information a fourth asset to be managed by the Entrepreneur.

There are many descriptions of the word, Entrepreneur. The Entrepreneur is defined as the bridge between labor and capital. He or she is considered as an owner or manager of a business who makes money through taking on risk and using one's initiative to help launch a new venture or enterprise, accepting full responsibility for the outcome.

Jean-Baptiste Say, the French Economist, is thought to have coined the word "Entrepreneur" in the 19th century, defining an Entrepreneur as "one who undertakes an enterprise, especially a contractor, acting as intermediary between capital and labour". Another definition by Say states: "The entrepreneur shifts economic resources out of lower and into higher productivity and greater yield".

So it all begins with the Entrepreneur and the Consumer and the Worker and the Land we live on. Economics began as a study of the Political Economy in Europe at a time when the world reached a point where international trade and sovereign competition lead to the discovery of the New World.

This lead to a need to discuss and examine and decide on systems for the efficient allocation of excess resources captured through colonialization and developed through systems of slavery:

The questions were the same as they are today. That's why we have so many Economists. We even have Conservative Economist and Liberal Economist, all asking the same questions. They are the same questions being asked in the halls of Congress and in the European Union today, and in every economy and every government: How can we create jobs and prosperity?
 What is the role of government in assisting and promoting the exchange of trade and commerce? What is the role of government in creating jobs?

What will be the economic conditions in the future? What is the role of banks in the economy and how much should they be regulated? What is the role of taxation, who pays and how do we decide what to spend it on? And finally, what's the way into a prosperous future? What works and what doesn't, and how can I get paid?

Kings to Constituents

Melanie admonished her son over his increased volume of self conversation and the noise he makes as he played with his toy car during our conversation. "Calm down a little bit, I'm trying to learn something here, and maybe you might get something out of it too", she said to him as he put his toy car on the floor and rolled it slowly, head down. He gets attitudes quickly, and let's them go just a fast.

"I just don't get it", Melanie continued, "I thought Economics was just supply and demand if I've got something you want, and you are willing to pay me what I want, or you're willing to bargain until we come to a price. And the government is just in the way, sometimes."

"The government is not… in the Way!", I said to her with fingers making a double quotation sign in the air, "Melanie, the government is the economy, or it is the context in which an economy functions".

I went on to tell her that there was a time when a single leader, a King or a Lord, ruled both the commerce and the people. In Europe in particular, people were held to the land by a system of Feudalism that basically acted as a form of forced labor, by legally restricting tenant farmers from moving from place to place, which is to some agree a form of slavery. And this was the system after the fall of the Roman Empire.

When the New World was discovered, the opportunity for individuals to expand their power over themselves became available to many Europeans. This freedom, this opportunity to function as an individual, was reinforced by the process of democratization of the English legal system into the United States of America.

When there were just Kings, the commercial and financial systems were controlled by the dictates of the King. Now that we have democracy, the decisions of individuals contribute to the rules and laws of the system.

So when democracy came along, economist included the influence of government, and government spending, and government taxation, in the framework of the determinable outcomes within the economy.

In America, voting is participating in the economy, and in the economic decisions that are made by the government. After Adam Smith, we had groups of economists called Neoclassical, Keynesians and Monetarists. You can learn more about these thinkers later on. But the thing to remember is, as governments became more democratic, and more people have been enfranchised, the right to vote is as much a contributor to the policies of spending and taxation as any dictate of a king. And this must be taken into consideration when making economic assessments of the potential of a future activity.

An example is the statement in the report of the Rating Agency after Debt Ceiling crisis in 2011, on lowering America's credit rating, that the caused was the inability of political adversaries to find common ground on those matters.

So as Adam Smith pointed out, the struggle between the Aristocrats and the worker is perpetual. The right to vote impacts all of that. So this is our history.

I sipped some tea and continued. I told Melanie that, before our chat, I had the occasion to read about a book entitled The New American Divide. I added that to the idea of democratic influences on economic policy. It's about a book by Charles Murray, the Brady Scholar at the American Enterprise Institute titled Coming Apart: The State of White America, 1960-2010. It describes the state of White America between 1960 and 2008, based upon an analysis of the demographic of White non-Hispanics in two distinct neighborhoods or hypothetical cities in the United States from 1960 to 2008. He chooses to end this inquiry in 2008 to eliminate any impacts of the recent recession. He also takes out all other people other than Whites. His point is to talk about the transition from a common culture in America, the values of marriage, work, and religion, a common set of values for rich and poor, in this now diverse society.

Today, he says, the working class differs from the elite in ways of life, from the diversity of high end products the wealthy can own and things they can do, as compared to the stable wages and life styles of the working class. Latte and pâté are not the same culture as a Miller High Life and a barbecue sandwich. Money, he argues, has created a disparity or gap between the commonality wealthy people once had with the working class.

Notwithstanding his perspective, from 1960 to 2008, he seems to forget the golden age of wealth at the turn of the last century, and cultural disparity between the very wealthy and the working class people in America then. His analysis is very interesting.

He talks about the extreme wealth difference that has taken place between 1960 and 2008 in hypothetical towns, one of which has historically been a wealthy upper-class neighborhood and the other historically being a neighborhood of working-class Whites. His point is that the change in culture in America has impacted marriage, single parenthood, industriousness, crime, and religiosity.

He picks these categories to indicate the impact on the reduction of marriage in a comparison between wealthy neighborhoods and working-class neighborhoods that has taken place over the last 50 years.

He reports that teen pregnancy has risen in the working-class neighborhoods while declining in the wealthy neighborhoods.

He speaks to the fact that the percentage of people working under 40 hours a week has increased in the poor neighborhoods, but has also increased in the wealthy ones as well. I might add that it could be that more wealthy people are working fewer hours for more compensation or reward while working-class people are working more for less wages, and there is more competition for working-class work.

He talks about the changes in the crime rates and how the wealthy neighborhoods have remained calm while the poor ones have seen increased crime activity.

He also suggests that the decline in participation in ritualistic religious organizations reflected in the decline in church attendance over this period has impacted philanthropy, and that the organized philanthropy of churches is a uniquely American way of reaching the poor. And of course, he disdains government support in every way.

This book is very interesting because the writer begins to rail against a system that has created the 1% per, or the wealthiest Aristocracy in American history, bigger than Rockefeller or J.P. Morgan, and bigger than Ford or IBM because all of this wealth is a shared asset. It's shared through investments by wealthy people, instead of Kings like in the old days, with anybody and everybody, since these investments are global in nature and seek the highest and best return, with the least risk. These people, Black, White, Asian, Arab, African, Chinese, Brazilian or Hungarian, they all have money and not parochial.

In a Wall Street Journal article of January 21, 2012, Murray wrote:

"The members of this elite have increasingly sorted themselves into hyper-wealthy and hyper-elite ZIP Codes that I call the SuperZIPs. In 1960, America already had the equivalent of SuperZIPs in the form of famously elite neighborhoods — places like the Upper East Side of New York, Philadelphia's Main Line, the North Shore of Chicago and Beverly Hills. But despite their prestige, the people in them weren't uniformly wealthy or even affluent. Across 14 of the most elite places to live in 1960, the median family income wasn't close to affluence. It was just $84,000 (in today's purchasing power). Only one in four adults in those elite communities had a college degree.

By 2000, that diversity had dwindled. Median family income had doubled, to $163,000 in the same elite ZIP Codes. The percentage of adults with B.A.s rose to 67% from 26%. And it's not just that elite neighborhoods became more homogeneously affluent and highly educated — they also formed larger and larger clusters.

If you are invited to a dinner party by one of Washington's power elite, the odds are high that you will be going to a home in Georgetown, the rest of Northwest D.C., Chevy Chase, Bethesda, Potomac or McLean, comprising 13 adjacent ZIP Codes in all.

If you rank all the ZIP Codes in the country on an index of education and income and group them by percentiles, you will find that 11 of these 13 D.C.-area ZIP Codes are in the 99th percentile and the other two in the 98th. Ten of them are in the top half of the 99th percentile.

Similarly large clusters of SuperZIPs can be found around New York City, Los Angeles, the San Francisco-San Jose corridor, Boston and a few of the nation's other largest cities. Because running major institutions in this country usually means living near one of these cities, it works out that the nation's power elite does in fact live in a world that is far more culturally rarefied and isolated than the world of the power elite in 1960.

And the isolation is only going to get worse. Increasingly, the people who run the country were born into that world. Unlike the typical member of the elite in 1960, they have never known anything but the new upper-class culture.

We are now seeing more and more third-generation members of the elite.

Not even their grandparents have been able to give them a window into life in the rest of America."

Mr. Murray makes key his point when he says, "White people, or the Common Man, in this country has been continuously voting against their own best interests by supporting the disparity that has occurred through the tax law changes between 1980 and the present day."

He suggests that some of the reasons for cultural disparity from the 1960's to the present are due to government programs and policies of the 60's that he says motivated people to not work and have kids out-of-wedlock because the government would take care of them. He's suggesting that White people are just as influenced as poor Blacks and Hispanics by the idea that government would give them money to not marry and have children, and would therefore promote something that these people would find more appealing than the self-discovery, self-respect, self-empowerment and control of their own lives that comes with getting a job.

And I wondered, what does the life or experiences of persons who are Black or Hispanic have to do with the lives of these White working-class people when the commonality they share is their economic status?

The ethnic comparison tells us nothing. You may as well choose English working-class people or Canadian's or such others as you may, but the only comparison should be with related conditions and experience, because nothing else matters to the issues of comparison. But that's my perspective.

He goes on further to criticize the idea that government is the solution and to continue to disparage government's potential for solving the problem.

And I said "Government is the solution if we say it's the solution. That's the American way."

He further points out that, "By 2000, that diversity had dwindled. Median family income had doubled, to $163,000 in the same elite ZIP Codes.

The percentage of adults with B.A.s rose to 67% from 26%.

And it's not just that elite neighborhoods became more homogeneously affluent and highly educated — they also formed larger and larger clusters."

He critics and analyses our society and its recent policies when he says, "As I've argued in much of my previous work, I think that the reforms of the 1960s jump-started the deterioration. Changes in social policy during the 1960s made it economically more feasible to have a child without having a husband if you were a woman or to get along without a job if you were a man;
safer to commit crimes without suffering consequences; and easier to let the government deal with problems in your community that you and your neighbors formerly had to take care of."

He goes on to suggest that the real problem is that "the elite of the elite" are not schmoozing with the hoi polloi.

He says the solution is for wealthy people to spend more time, they and their children, with the people in the poor neighborhoods or working-class sections of the society so that they can become culturally indoctrinated in the ways of the Common Man, and so that we will have a similar cultural affinity to each other.

For this is the basis of his whole book, that is to say that we are now in the midst of a cultural inequality between the very wealthy and the Common Man. His solutions are very simple. No government intervention.

He says, "The only thing that can make a difference is the recognition among Americans of all classes that a problem of cultural inequality exists and that something has to be done about it. That "something" has nothing to do with new government programs or regulations. Public policy has certainly affected the culture, unfortunately, but unintended consequences have been as grimly inevitable for conservative social engineering as for liberal social engineering."

So this gentleman has made a point which is in conflict with his premise. By suggesting that wealthy people, those in the top 1% of the nation's personal wealth, are the only ones who can solve the disparity between the wealthy and the not-so-wealth, and can do so by having an association with Joe the Plumber forgets that the disparity is the problem.

The point this book really makes is that there has been a change in the population of the United States, between 1960 and 2008, that has impacted White working-class people just as it has impacted nonwhite working-class people.

And, that it has demonstrated that the policies promoted by conservative politicians that sell social issues and social engineering to the White working-class has not solved their economic problems or promoted their incomes, while those of the top tier have been rising during this period.

The government finances the economic activities needed by the society that the private sector either will not do or that only government can do. Things like wars or the Tennessee Valley Authority or Hoover Dam or coordinating the completion of the

Transcontinental Railroad, things like that. Or things like Social

Security and Medicare. Government often facilitates economic

growth and private sector opportunity through research or pilot

programs or infrastructure funding. In one way or another, the

people decide what is in their best interests and it is time that

determines whether or not they've made the right choices.

I think the author has hit on something, but it escapes him. A

percentage of the White demographic of working-class people

continually votes against their own interests, supporting policies

and candidates who have no more concern for their economic

interest than the Wall Street Banker in New York who sells toxic

assets to off-shore buyers.

This is a natural consequence of the changes in societies that Adam

Smith pointed out in his book. Those who have more have

increased their wealth to the level at which an annual income of

$250,000 in the year 2000 would constitute being in the top 1-2 % of

the nation's households.

Today, it takes $397,000 to be in that number. The top 1% of the people own 40% of the nation's wealth or 70% of the nation's financial assets, by some accounts today. This can be better understood when you find that the US has moved to 2nd in the world, after South Africa, in low-wage workers as a percentage of the workforce.

"It's like we are all in this together", I touted. like it or not, because we are living in an interconnectness and linkage that stretches from me to you to the six degrees of separation, and we are all in touch, on time, tuned in and turned on through the Internet and all its …What Not! We are the world, from now on.

Now don't forget, we set this sucker up with the invention of the Atomic Bomb and all that is still out there. We have that and we have global warming, and the population boom, and terrorist and all that. So, we have lots to be economical about."

What's Our Stake?

"How interesting, Melanie tilted her head and sang, "Maybe you can tell us how to understand the European financial crisis and how the problems in America were exported through toxic assets, like mortgages that were bundled together."

We were chatting about all of that, along with questions about who's doing what, when Bret reminded us that he was in the room.

"So, what does that have to do with us?" he asked as if he was in the discussion. But how do you talk about the American Economy with a 5-year old kid and give something to the conversation that Melanie and I want to talk about? I started talking about the history of the country and how important it is to the understanding of any human endeavor.

"What's past is prologue", I blurted out to Bret, "Remember? That was written on the National Archives. Bret, you saw that, remember?"

I started by talking about the American Economic system and how it began, and was developed, with and through a system of slavery, as a way to really show him how we got to this democratic free-market economy. Ours is a system that grew out of what existed when the economic and political forces that affect the economy in this democracy began to aggregate.

Bret looked directly at me, waiting for an answer as he twirled his toy car around his finger beside his head.

"Bret, don't do that", Melanie said sternly, "That thing will fly out of your hand and hit somebody. Now, you wouldn't want that, would you?" He stopped and turned to me and said, "What about us in America? Is the economy going to get us, too?" I turned to Melanie as we laughed and said, "I hope so"!

"It's all about banks, Melanie. When the government began to regulate banks, things started to happen. In the old days, banks were private collections of money that Merchants used to facilitate trade.

A bank in one place could offer a Note that could be used to get paid in another place. Yes, banks printed money, that's what the Notes were used for. These "relationships" allowed trade and commerce to take place during the Mercantile period, just before the discovery of America. But soon, banks began to control money and the Kings were affected by the comparative wealth and influence that they couldn't control. So, banks and government began to cooperate since many Kings borrowed from private banks to finance development and wars in Europe before America was discovered. Today, we have a bank crisis in America, and in Europe, and we have had them throughout the history of the world."

"Here", I continued, "Here's something I found on the web that might help clear things up."

The Panic of 1819 was America's first global financial crisis, triggering the changes and tensions to come in the America following the Revolution and the complete separation from the rule of England.

This was long before the Keynesians of the 20th century and the Monetarist that followed the Classical Economist like Adam Smith. This was a time when the role of government in financial markets was being created, like it or not. Since new institutions bring new influences and movements in the marketplace, new institutions required new methods. The Panic of 1819 is important in understanding the economics of this democratic nation because it was the first real economic crisis in America.

There were three key causes of the Panic of 1819, inflation, public debt from the War of 1812 and the Louisiana Purchase. The Panic had a lasting effect on the American banking system and directed attention to the crucial 1819-1821 session of Congress where changes and attempted changes to American financial policies would foster Southern sectionalism and lead to the American Civil War.

The Second Bank of the United States was chartered by the U.S. government in 1816. It was set up to help manage the federal debt left by the War of 1812 (1812–14) and to curb inflation brought on by unregulated state banks.

In the early nineteenth century there was no standardized national currency. Instead, because most banks were privately owned and operated for commercial purposes, they issued their own paper money.

Prices throughout the United States had been rising dramatically since shortly after the end of the War of 1812, mostly caused by the United States government's attempt to pay off the war debt. Since the war debt was mostly held by Americans, payment in currency, now deflated in value, was legal. In 1816 the Second Bank of the United States was formed, but it continued to feed the expansion by having significantly more money in circulation than it did gold reserves.

Effectively, this paper money was a promise to pay in gold or silver on demand, an action known in financial markets as Specie. Specie is the precious metal standard or backup the paper currency represents, like gold or silver. These banks were necessary in order to supply the credit needed to buy land, finance businesses, and create economic growth.

However, they tended to lend more paper "money" than they had the Specie to cover. Therefore, if several large creditors demanded payment in cash at the same time, the result was called a "run" and usually led to the bank's failure. If several banks failed at the same time the result was a financial panic. This happened in the panics of 1819 and 1837. Both of these events led to high rates of inflation and national depressions.

The Second Bank of the United States faced many of the problems that plagued state institutions. Between 1816 and 1818, for instance, dishonest managers of the Baltimore, Maryland, branch of the Second Bank swindled investors out of more than $1 million before they were caught. The following year this scandal forced the resignation of Bank President William Jones.

The reputation of the Second Bank was restored by Jones' successor, a South Carolina lawyer named Langdon Cheves. Cheves brought discipline to the Bank's dealings, sharply reducing the number of loans issued and aggressively pursuing individuals and banks that defaulted on loans.

Cheves' policies helped place the Bank on a sound financial footing, however, they also caused a number of bank failures that led directly to the Panic of 1819.

Beginning in 1818, the bank moved from an expansionary stance to a deflationary stance to combat the rampant inflation and to pay off the nearly 4 million dollar debt associated with the Louisiana Purchase. Since this debt was mostly held by people outside the United States it could not be paid by inflated currency. It had to be paid out of the species reserves, which were very low in relationship to the currency outstanding.

To increase its specie reserves, the bank switched from what is generally characterized as a pro-inflation stance to a pro-deflation mode in July, 1818, although the managers did not foresee the massive contraction their movement from paper currency to hard currency would create.

By curtailing the outflow of hard currency in 1818, the Second Bank of the United States significantly reduced the ability of the state banks to stay solvent. In essence, this movement curtailed expansion over the next year and put pressure on the state banks.

First in the system to have problems was the state bank of Kentucky, probably the weakest bank in the system at that time. Other banks, mostly in the West and South also had problems. Anti-bank sentiment rose throughout the United States.

One of the ways the United States raised money before The Civil War was the sale of public land, thus making the voters into debtors in this democracy. There were so many of these debtors that they could influence politicians, who in turn proposed debtor relief bills in Congress. In his 1820 address to Congress, President Monroe got on the bandwagon, endorsing the third and most substantial debt relief package. A month later, Secretary of the Treasury William Crawford laid out the details for relief of the debtors. Two months later the bills were passed and signed by the President.

The result was chaos. Suddenly debtors realized their political power and set about to relieve more of their debt on a state level. However, problems arose in the disbursement of the relief. In a lot of cases the original land owner had sold all or a portion of the land without paying off the original debt. Should the debt relief be paid to the original owner or current owner? In general, states in the South and West passed debt relief measures while Northern states held back some or all of these laws. In the end the non-speculative public became responsible to foot the bill for the debt-laden speculators. That's America.

As land was sold to pay debts the price began to fall, precipitating a drop in general prices. The South, a one-crop economy, was devastated as cotton prices were cut in half in two years, between 1818 and 1820. Western expansion was blocked when the U. S. government stopped work on the National Road.

With the price of land depressed and the United States in need of cash, it sought more land to sell. One of the ways to get this land was through the annexation of states.

When a territory became a state it would normally turn over an agreed on number of acres to the United States, which in turn would sell the land to raise cash.

In 1820, Missouri and Maine were annexed under the Missouri Compromise, a first step to Statehood. From 1819 to 1821, the economy was in a recession. In 1821 it began to grow again, although it would be until 1823 before this growth could be considered healthy.

In 1832 the Presidential election year, Henry Clay and Daniel Webster, two of Jackson's most vocal opponents in Congress, decided to challenge the President. Even though the Bank's charter was not due to expire for four years, they promoted a bill that renewed the charter of the Second Bank of the United States. Clay and Webster believed that, whether Jackson signed the bill into law, the President would alienate a significant number of voters and risk his chance of a second term. Jackson vetoed the bill on July 10, 1832, in one of the most strongly worded messages ever sent to

Congress. Although Clay tried to make the veto an issue in his campaign for the presidency later that year, Jackson easily won reelection, defeating Clay by a margin of 219 electoral votes to 49.

Jackson believed his reelection represented a mandate from the American people to destroy the Second Bank of the United States. In 1833 he instructed his Secretary of the Treasury, Louis McLane, to prepare for the expiration of the Bank's charter by removing the government's deposits to certain state institutions, known as "pet banks." McLane refused and was moved to the position of Secretary of State. His successor, William Duane, also refused and resigned. Jackson did not find a pliable Secretary of the Treasury until former Attorney General Roger B. Taney took the position.

The removal of the government's deposits brought Jackson into conflict with Nicholas Biddle, who was as strong-willed as the President. Biddle felt that Jackson's actions exceeded his constitutional authority and tried to force the President to renew the Second Bank's charter by sharply reducing the number of loans and by vigorously collecting outstanding debts.

Biddle's actions, however, failed to deter the President. Biddle succeeded only in causing a financial crisis for American business in the summer and autumn of 1834. Worse, he alienated some of his strongest supporters.

For his part, Jackson made a determined effort to eliminate the extension of credit by forbidding banks with federal deposits from issuing banknotes of less than $5 denominations. In 1836 he issued the presidential order known as the Specie Circular, which required purchasers of public lands to pay in cash.

By the time Jackson left office the Second Bank of the United States credit system had been severely crippled. The Specie Circular was the final salvo in the Bank War, which ended in victory for Jacksonian principles.

When the Bank's charter expired in 1836, it sought and received a charter from Pennsylvania, the state in which the main branch of the Bank had always been housed. It then operated under the name of the United States Bank of Pennsylvania. In 1839 the Bank found itself with too little specie to cover its loans. It went into receivership and was dissolved in 1841.

Jackson's victory left a questionable legacy. A boom in public works, such as canal construction, manufacturing, cotton production, and land sales, followed Jackson's decision to remove funds from the Second Bank of the United States. However, soon after his hand-picked successor Martin Van Buren took over in 1837, the country experienced a severe depression, marked by high rates of inflation and large public debt that lasted for nearly a decade. Many historians argue that by eliminating the Second Bank of the United States, Jackson removed an institution that might have eased the Panic of 1837.

"And that was just the beginning", I said to Melanie. Bret rolled his car over my shoe and made some noises.

Banks are People, Too

I turned from my laptop and said, "So, what have we learned?"

Melanie shrugged and said, "What!?"

I told her we learned banks are people too. If a corporation is a

person, then banks are people too.

"Mitt Romney said so while on the campaign trail, remember?"

Corporations are people, my friend, he said on the stump, referring

to the US Supreme Court decision in the landmark case, Citizens

United v. Federal Elections Commission, where money was

declared free speech and corporations were declared to be persons.

And just like people, they make and have economic interests.

We had a financial crisis, a global financial crisis in 2007 and 2008.

That crisis continues to this day. When the housing bubble burst in

2006, this caused the value of securities to fall rapidly, causing a

domino effect. Why did securities fall?

Securities are like dollar bills. They are a promise to pay a particular amount of money or something so you don't have to carry that money or something around.

A security says I secure the value of that asset where ever it may be, and you can claim it under certain conditions. That means I can sell that piece of paper, that value of an asset, without having to move the asset, and I can trade or exchange this piece of paper for the money that equals the rights to that asset. The monies in the banks are backed by Species. With Securities, Investment Banks and other investment houses must have collateral to back up whatever paper they issue, be it gold or other currencies or mortgages or properties or rights to things. Them's the rules.

The recent financial crisis, the banking crisis and mortgage crisis and all those other crises were evaluated by the US Financial Crisis Inquiry Commission which released their report in January of 2011 and concluded that "the crisis was avoidable and was caused by several interlinked activities and policy failures, from widespread failures in financial regulation, including the Federal Reserve's failure to stem the tide of toxic mortgages.

Another factor was the dramatic breakdowns in corporate governance including too many financial firms acting recklessly and taking too much risk, along with an explosive mix of excessive borrowing and risk by households and Wall Street Bankers that put the financial system on a collision course with the crisis. In general, many significant policy makers were ill-prepared for the crisis, lacking a full understanding of the financial system they oversaw and there were systematic breaches in accountability and ethics at every level.

So what happened with the banks? It is suggested that a significant increase in savings was made available to investors during the 2002 to 2007 period, so a lot of money was looking for something to do. This was also a time when Brazil and India and China were competing with the United States and Europe for the oil energy needed for economic growth. There were many factors happening at this time, notwithstanding that the American economy was doing pretty good. Things weren't bad.

When the "Global Pool of Money" was increased by a significant amount in fixed income securities from these new emerging market sources and sovereign investment funds, it rose from 36 trillion in 2002 to 70 trillion in 2007. This pool increased as savings from high-growth developing nations entered global capital markets. Brazil, India and China, and the new emerging African nations contributed to this increase in opportunities for investments overseas.

In America, the real estate industry was thriving. Not only were people receiving below prime rate loans, but people were receiving above prime rate loans in large numbers which fueled the speculation in real estate that occurred during this period. When the bubble burst in the real estate market, it diminished the value of the mortgages that were written as collateral for loans to other borrowers, under the assumption that the mortgages would pay in full over a fixed period of time.

Banks have rules. They have to have a certain percentage of reserves or specie held in the bank, and not loaned out, in relation to the total volume of loans that they make. This is called a Reserve.

The Federal Reserve is the Reserve bank of the United States.

So the bubble burst over here and we had the recession. Many factors contributed to the recession, but the decline in the housing and real estate markets caused a decline in the construction industries and all of the related industries to that. This impacted consumers, government and the banking system since it effected every aspect of how business is done. One of the things pointed out in the report of January 2011 was the fact that decisions made by people were the primary cause of all of the impacts.

Whether it was due to a lack of oversight, a lack of inquiry, a lack of experience, or a lack of awareness, all of these factors contributed. Oversight and insight and accountability are the remedies. Today we have a crisis in Greece, which is a crisis in Europe, because it is a crisis in the banks that loan money to Greece, and other countries, adding to the stress on those banks because they do not have sufficient reserves, since some of their collateral is based on toxic assets such as bundled mortgage packages that are half their face value.

So, if the value of the reserves goes down, the amount of money that can be loaned goes down, causing a restriction in the credit markets.

I tapped along on the laptop, and in the silence, I began to notice that Bret was making more noise and sounds as he moved his toy car into a collision with his Transformer. But he calmed down as I begin to talk again.

I pointed out to Melanie an article I found that was in the Wall Street Journal on June 27, 2011. This article was entitled GLOBAL BANKING IS WHAT'S REALLY IN CRISIS. It was by Erwin Stelzer. In this article he talks about an international banking crisis and compares Greece to Lehman Brothers in our crisis. Too big to fail is a phrase that keeps coming up. In the case of Greece, he contends that "Greece was not too big to fail, but too interconnected to the international banking system, too interconnected to the political ambitions of those who have spent decades replacing the system of nation states with a united Europe." He points out that Greek banks held 99.3 billion of their government's sovereign debt.

He said, "The Economist estimates that if Greek banks were required to recognize the fact that markets are valuing Greek government debt at about half the value assigned to this paper on their books, shareholders would be wiped out and the banks would have to scramble to raise substantial new capital."

I hit the keys of the laptop and swirled my finger on the mouse pad and said to Melanie, "Here's something I think makes the picture clearer".

In this article on the global banking crisis, Mr. Stelzer says it well. 'Greece's problem has also revealed another crisis-a crisis in government. The Tower of Babel that is euroland governance is collapsing. Markets have gone from puzzled to incredulous and on to near- panic as Herman Van Rompuy (the first time president of the European Council) says one thing, Jose Manual Barros (the 11th and current president of the European Commission) another, Jean-Claude Trichet (who was the president of the European Central Bank, a position he held from 2003 to 2011.

He is also a member of the Board of Directors of the Bank for International Settlements. In 2008, Trichet ranked fifth on *Newsweek*'s list of the world's most powerful), Angela Merkel still another. Their failure to sing from the same hymn sheet is damaging – no, destroying – any confidence markets might once have had in the confidence of the euro zone governing class. "

" I say again, Melanie", I told her, Banks are people too. "

But the world is changing. The world is becoming more global and the banking system is leading the way. International trade began to thrive when the banking system was refined in Holland as the European powers struggled for colonial control in the 1700's. In those days, there were no instant global transfers of funds in astounding amounts. There was no international paper such as the toxic assets that were bundled and sold to European banks which exacerbated the crisis that arose when these banks held debt from sovereign governments that was overvalued.

How did this Sovereign Debt get here? What happened in Greece? A lot of this has to do with identity, European nations and politicians inside and outside of the European Union, posturing and politicking for personal interests. In addition, the Greek crisis is a crisis in the structure of the economy. There has been a lack of economic growth in Europe, and the European population is aging and increasingly consists of immigrants.

And Europe is settled with one more problem, if you're in the European Union, as a sovereign state, you can't print money as a country on your own as a monetary tool to fight inflation or pay debts. The printing of money is inflationary, if done by itself, because it adds more cash supply to a stable demand which means prices will rise because there's more money than demand. That said, in any case money cannot be printed by member countries on their own. It's like being Texas in the United States. They can't print money, only the Fed can.

In today's world, the developing nations will receive most of the new banking activities taking place on a global basis, in emerging economies in Africa, Asia and Latin America that are largely free of the debt and deleveraging that has undermined growth in the West. These emerging economies remain among the few areas where growth is taking place. Statistics from the Bank of International Settlements show that, in 2011, European and other cross-border lending to emerging economies had declined by $75 billion, indicating the greatest decline since the Lehman collapse in 2008. Within three months, the same report showed a reverse cross-border lending to emerging economies in the first quarter of 2012 as having increased by $86 billion. Japanese banks, Chinese banks, Korean banks moved in to fill the void occurred because the European banks had to withdraw to service the euro zone.

So, today we have come out of a banking restructuring over the last three or four decades, a restructuring in which bank consolidation has taken place. We have a global transfer of funds on a daily basis at the speed of light in the trillions of dollars.

You can get a loan with a smart phone and send it to another part of the world. Many banks have merged as a result of the new legislation passed to facilitate financial system operations or to just make money.

You'll notice that the small-town neighborhood bank has somewhat disappeared, along with savings-and-loan organizations. You may also notice that there are still a few banks that are, "too big to fail", and that they are the same ones that not only initiated the banking crisis but are gaining from the improving economy. So there you have it.

Class Warfare

"And now", Melanie asked, "What's up with all this struggle between the politicians about taxes. What's fair? Should we let the rich people stop paying taxes since they are the ones who create jobs?"

"You sound like you believe in class warfare", I chimed in.

"I believe in having class", she smiled and said. And at that moment, Bret asked the question, "Ma, what is class warfare?" Melanie and I looked at each other and smiled as I pondered how to answer that question and still keep his attention. I took a shot at it.

The Economic Elite, who are sometimes called the Oligarchy, provide a significant Leading Sector anchor for the economy and incorporates workers or job holders as part of its economic impact. Yet, with all its might, the Economic Elite do not employ the majority of the job holders in the economy.

That distinction goes to what is referred to as Small Business, enterprises that supplement, support and feed on the Leading Sector, as well as the non-commercial sector (churches, non-profits, NGO's, etc.) that serves the community.

The difference between the Economic Elite and the Common Man (workers or employees) is that the Elite cannot be the Elite without the working people while the working people, and the poor, can sustain that status on their own. It's called subsistence and the Elite cannot be themselves at the subsistence level.

Can't happen.

This Economic Elite consist of Investors and Entrepreneurs in the industries that drive the economy, the Leading Sector, who oversee the major industries and control the Leading Sectors in the economy. This Economic Elite changes over time due to wars, new technologies, discoveries and changes in competitive advantage, as does the composition of the people in it. From cotton to railroads to automobiles to computers to credit default swaps and music, the

Leading Sector provides the spark and focus of the economy. This is called "competitive advantage" when you make something better or cheaper than the competition.

And, no matter what the Leading Sector is, it will always contain a fixed or relatively stable level of workers. Employment for that Leading Sector will incorporate as many jobs as it can until a level of Equilibrium is reached is reached. In other words, you will hire autoworkers until you can't sell another car. You'll continue until you have enough workers to make enough cars to sell all the cars people are going to buy, every day, every year.

It's Small Business that generates additional economic activity, from cottage industry to the lunch truck or the beauty parlor or the street vendor at the subsistence level of the economy, while serving workers needs, industries needs, and the needs of the non-commercial sectors.

This economic array of small business, from the lemonade stand or the window washers to manufacturers and service providers, feeds from and circulates with the Leading Sectors of the economy, much like the planets move around the Sun.

That's where the economy grows. In either case, the infrastructure of government greases the wheel and creates the stability in the economy necessary to create a job, and the Government Sector hires workers as well.

"We need to know a couple of terms to keep going", I said. "An Oligopoly is defined as a small number of sellers: an economic condition in which there are so few suppliers of a product that one supplier's actions can have a significant impact on prices and on its competitors. An Oligarchy is defined as a small governing group: a small group of people who together govern a nation or control an organization, often for their own purposes.

Oligarchies are the people and institutions at the top of the social, political and economic pyramid who have power that comes from their position in the economy. In the US, people have upward mobility which changes the makeup of the Oligarchy over time, and will continue to do so.

That's the beauty of our system. With the Supreme Court declaration in the Citizen's United case, which defined corporations as persons, the influence on government is a lot more likely to be effected by the Oligarchy due to the increased influence of money. With that influence, it is possible to influence the direction of the economy. This will always, eventually, run into the democracy.

We saw a similar situation when President Theodore Roosevelt became the "Trust Buster" in 1901, bringing the Moguls into line with the economy. The needs of the Common Man and the Working Class were subjugated to moneyed interest. Money ruled the day until Roosevelt passed several Anti-Trust Laws and other regulatory measures to limit the power of the oligarchy.

Today, we have corporations as people. However, logic tells us that, if a corporation can create another corporation, either with another corporation or without, anyone and everyone can create a corporation. Eventually, we will each and all bypass the measures to regulate campaign spending by forming corporations, since people are persons too. And we will pool our money and have an impact.

The Corporate World is already engaged in advocating for its position on behalf of the "Have's" and their interest as I related to Melanie in an experience that I thought would help make my point about the power of money in the democracy. On Sunday July 15th, I watched Larry Kudlow on the CNN program GPS with Fareed Zakaria when he spoke these words in response to an inquiry into the politics of the day:" Privatize Everything". This is the policy and ideology of the new Free Market Movement.

The Free Market and free enterprise system is under attack, they say. Some believe government's role should be limited in the economy.

Arthur Brooks, head of the American Enterprise Institute in Washington, DC and author of the book, "The Road to Freedom: How to Win the Fight for Free Enterprise" promotes the idea that government should not get involved when market failures occur. He says that the government shouldn't get involved every time there is an oil spill like the Gulf of Mexico in 2010. If the government can do anything about it, he says, the government cannot do it cost –effectively

He believes that government is not the solution, "it's the problem" and the government that governs least, governs best, as a "statement of principle". But nothing he said demonstrated that Free Enterprise was in jeopardy, nor that government constraints serve the general welfare by governing least. Or allowing the uncertainty and chaos that would come from a lack of government investment, regulation and oversight, and no agreement as to what constitutes order in the economy. Conservative philosophy promotes the idea that the Free Enterprise system is somehow connected to the size of government.

The Free Enterprise, free market system is really about the ability of the individual to be free of the impact of government on his or her ability to engage in commerce. Freedom to engage in commerce is a freedom in America that comes from the Constitution, establishing individual freedom and Civil Rights.

Civil rights allows people to redress issues between themselves, in an open court, with those with whom they do business. Without the government, there is chaos. You cannot have a Free Enterprise system without regulation. We are lucky that the free enterprise system in this democracy allows us to work together to find solutions to problems. So, once again, the key to the free enterprise system is the ability of the people, through a government of full representation, to promote the general welfare and secure the blessings of peace for us and our posterity. This creates economic stability.

The role of government in the class struggle, the fight over wages and prices and government oversight and "Laissey Faire" is the role of an arbitrator or judge between the power of money and the power of numbers.

Without democracy, economic balance is elusive.

Evidence comes from a 2011 study by the US Congressional Budget Office wherein it was discovered that the top earning 1 percent of households gained about 275% after federal taxes and income transfers over a period between 1979 and 2007, compared to a gain of just under 40% for the 60 percent in America's middle income distribution.

It's notable that the share of total income going to the top 1% of American households (also after federal taxes and income transfers) increased from 11.3% in 1979 to 20.9% in 2007. Research indicates that, from 1992 to 2007, the top 400 earners in the United States saw their incomes increase 392% and their average tax rate reduced by 37%.

During the Great Recession of 2007-2009, inequality declined, with total income going to the bottom 99 percent of Americans declining by 11.6%, but falling faster (36.3%) for the top 1%. However, the disparity in income increased again during the 2009-2010 recovery, with the top 1% of income earners capturing 11.6% of income and capital gains, and the income of the other 99% remained flat, growing by only 0.2%.

So what does this say? It says tax increases for wealthy people do not lead to jobs. The government has a role to play. The government is the people.

"We need to know a couple of terms to keep going, I said, an Oligopoly is defined as a small number of sellers: an economic condition in which there are so few suppliers of a product that one supplier's actions can have a significant impact on prices and on its competitors. An Oligarchy is defined as a small governing group: a small group of people who together govern a nation or control an organization, often for their own purposes.

Oligarchies are the people and institutions at the top of the social, political and economic pyramid who have power that comes from their position in the economy.

In the US, people have upward mobility which changes the makeup of the Oligarchy over time, and will continue to do so. That's the beauty of our system. With the Supreme Court declaration in the Citizen's United case, which defined corporations as persons, the influence on government is a lot more likely to be effected by the Oligarchy due to the increased influence of money. With that influence, it is possible to influence the direction of the economy. This will always, eventually, run into the democracy.

We saw a similar situation when President Theodore Roosevelt became the "Trust Buster" in 1901, bringing the Moguls into line with the economy. The needs of the Common Man and the Working Class were subjugated to moneyed interest. Money ruled the day until Roosevelt passed several Anti-Trust Laws and other regulatory measures to limit the power of the oligarchy. Today, we have corporations as people. However, logic tells us that, if a corporation can create another corporation, either with another corporation or without, anyone and everyone can create a corporation.

Eventually, we will each and all bypass the measures to regulate campaign spending by forming corporations, since people are persons too.

I related an experience to Melanie that I thought would help make my point. On Sunday July 15th, I watched Larry Kudlow on the CNN program GPS with Fareed Zakaria when he spoke these words in response to an inquiry into the politics of the day:" Privatize Everything". This is the policy and ideology of the new Free Market Movement.

The Free Market and free enterprise system is under attack, they say. Some believe government's role should be limited in the economy. Arthur Brooks, head of the American Enterprise Institute and author of the book, "The Road to Freedom: How to Win the Fight for Free Enterprise" promotes the idea that government should not get involved when market failures occur.

He says that the government shouldn't get involved every time there is an oil spill like the Gulf of Mexico in 2010. If the government can do anything about it, he says, the government cannot do it cost –effectively

He believes that government is not the solution, "it's the problem" and the government that governs least, governs best, as a "statement of principle". But nothing he said demonstrated that Free Enterprise was in jeopardy, nor that government constraints serve the general welfare by governing least or allowing the uncertainty and chaos that would come from a lack of government investment, regulation and oversight and no agreement as to what constitutes order in the economy. Conservative philosophy promotes the idea that the Free Enterprise system is somehow connected to the size of government.

The Free Enterprise, free market system is really about the ability of the individual to be free of the impact of government on his or her ability to engage in commerce. Freedom to engage in commerce is a freedom in America that comes from the Constitution, establishing individual freedom and Civil Rights.

Civil rights allows people to redress issues between themselves, in an open court, with those with whom they do business. Without the government, there is chaos. You cannot have a Free Enterprise system without regulation. We are lucky that the free enterprise system in this democracy allows us to work together to find solutions to problems. So, once again, the key to the free enterprise system is the ability of the people, through a government of full representation, to promote the general welfare and secure the blessings of peace for us and our posterity. This creates economic stability.

Evidence comes from a 2011 study by the US Congressional Budget Office wherein it was discovered that the top earning 1 percent of households gained about 275% after federal taxes and income transfers over a period between 1979 and 2007, compared to a gain of just under 40% for the 60 percent in America's middle income distribution. It's notable that the share of total income going to the top 1% of American households (also after federal taxes and income transfers) increased from 11.3% in 1979 to 20.9% in 2007.

Research indicates that, from 1992 to 2007, the top 400 earners in the United States saw their incomes increase 392% and their average tax rate reduced by 37%.

During the Great Recession of 2007-2009, inequality declined, with total income going to the bottom 99 percent of Americans declining by 11.6%, but falling faster (36.3%) for the top 1%. However, the disparity in income increased again during the 2009-2010 recovery, with the top 1% of income earners capturing 11.6% of income and capital gains, and the income of the other 99% remained flat, growing by only 0.2%.

So what does this say? It says tax increases for wealthy people do not lead to jobs. The government has a role to play. The government is the people.

What's Free Enterprise?

Almost as soon as I finished my last word on the matter, Bret had

another question. He wanted to know what free enterprise means,

by asking the question, "Ma, What is Free Enterprise?

Bret's question stirred my memory of a conversation I recently had

about this concept. I reminisced on it as I described it to Melanie.

I sat at a bar not long ago and met an interesting man who drank

only American beer and snacked on peanuts as we watched a soccer

match on television that featured his favorite team in the European

Soccer League. He was a stocky, dark-eyed Latin-American and a

strong smile that produced deep lines in his face, and a deep

compassionate expression in the eyes. He was an older man with

wispy white hair that was Einstein-like and flowed in breezes

around his head. He wore thin-rimmed glasses and was well

dressed in casual Saturday afternoon attire for the early autumn.

His name was Rodrigo and he told me he was a university professor

with a motivated interest in our country from his educational

experience here.

He was an investor in the American economy as the owner of a restaurant with his extended family in New York, and was in Washington, DC on vacation prior to his return home. He and I meandered through sports and cultural inquiries in the few moments between glances at the Soccer match on TV, and we soon came to a conversation about politics, American politics in a political year.

With his slight accent, he brought some things to my attention that led me to do some research on the matter. His voice was soft with a sharp tone deep inside that spoke of confidence in his positions. With his energy and amplified manner of relating to you, he was fun to be with as well.

His argument was this, that from the Jackson Administration to the Civil War, through all efforts against integration, a population of rural poor and working White men were given "privilege", through segregation and anti-immigrant laws as a method of maintaining an economic caste system following the abolition of slavery.

In a society that required a reward for complicity in that system, my friend argued that this clarifies the reason for the enfranchisement of White men who didn't own land.

I told Melanie that I was lead to a search for the history of the enfranchisement of White males in America because of that conversation about White men in this country who couldn't vote if they didn't own land. Rodrigo told me that the enfranchisement of White men in America was a long term proposition that took almost 50 years from the rime of the Constitution in 1776 to the 1840's.

The connection of the vote to White privilege had lead to the continuous acceptance and support of a population of poor to working class White men for slavery and the oppression of minorities and immigrants that followed. Rodrigo said to me, "White privilege or White Supremacy cannot exist without the presence of Black people." This was his argument since a very small percentage of Whites actually owned slaves.

This all arose with a News story that was airing during the half-time report. It spoke to the voting in a 2012 Republican Primary election that commented on the decisive female vote that made the difference in that specific contest. It was the 19st Amendment that gave women the right to vote and how things have changed since then. My new friend commented that women could vote in New England until that policy was reversed in the decades after the Revolution. This led us to a discussion on the Black vote.

Rodrigo's view is that slavery was a labor-control system that restricted wages by artificially lowering the cost for workers, eliminating competition for employment and providing surpluses at no cost to the employer. He said that, from about 1836, the enfranchisement of White men, based solely on being of European ancestry, non-African or Indian, was expanding in the law. A connection between non-landed White men to the classes of land owners and educated men evolved as well. This provided a reliable political "base" for causes that supported the interest of landowners, robber barons, industrialist and educated elitist men.

The Ku Klan was built upon links between the Oligopoly of the Confederacy and the landless workers and poor farmers."White Privilege" often came into confrontation when the interest of White working-class labor collided with the interest of the landed class.

These issues brought forth alliances that challenged the benefits of White Supremacy, since the majority of the population consisted of workers and farmers, leading to unions, the right of women to vote, and the nation we have today.

From this encounter, I began a search to help understand the reasons for the current political divide, wherein some White men vote against their own personal, economic and political interest when it comes from the apparent opposition. America must understand itself to better itself and to improve on the economic decisions we must make. This is what .lead me to the books and articles I mention here.

Through my search I discovered that there is no right to vote in the United States Constitution, so each state's standards have evolved separately unless federal laws were passed that applied to every state. When this country was founded, only White men with property were routinely permitted to vote (although freed African Americans could vote in four states). Landless White working-class men, almost all women, and all other people of color were denied the franchise.

By the time of the Civil War, most White men were allowed to vote, whether or not they owned property, thanks to the efforts of those who championed the cause of frontiersmen and White immigrants (who had to wait 14 years for citizenship and the right to vote, in some cases). Literacy tests, poll taxes, and even religious tests were used in various places, and most White women, people of color, and Native Americans still could not vote.

The movement to enfranchise has been long in coming for un-landed White males.

White men have been discriminated against as un-landed, non property owner people since the era of the European Kings.

In America, the White male vote was a gift from the landed and property ownership interests to a demographic of voters which allows them to "feel" that they have privilege and "superior" status as a result of the physical and cultural position of their race in the world. This perception is the key to an identity that is partially, if not completely defined in comparison to others who don't have the same freedoms. It was a "pecking order" identity defined by law.

A short lesson in history tells us that King Henry VI of England established the rule that only male owners of property worth at least forty shillings, a significant sum, were entitled to vote in England in 1432. The rules for boroughs were complex, but also restrictive. Changes were made to the system through major reforms in the Reform Act 1832.

Suffrage in the United Kingdom was slowly changed over the 19th and 20th centuries through the use of the Reform Acts and the Representation of the People Acts, resulting in universal suffrage, excluding children and convicted prisoners.

My research found that, in America, the Revolutionary War stimulated a desire for reform. Advocates of change said that the conflict was about liberty and representation. They believed in a voting system that embodied those aims for more people. Debates continued to intensify between 1776 and the adoption of the federal Constitution in 1789. The primary concern focused on extending voting rights to veterans, the implications of a broader electorate, and the validity of property requirements. Property requirements seemed to attract the most attention. They came under attack almost as soon as the Revolution began.

On this subject, Benjamin Franklin wrote:

Today a man owns a jackass worth 50 dollars and he is entitled to vote; but before the next election the jackass dies. The man in the mean time has become more experienced, his knowledge of the principles of government, and his acquaintance with mankind, are more extensive, and he is therefore better qualified to make a proper selection of rulers – but the jackass is dead and the man cannot vote. Now gentlemen, pray inform me, in whom is the right of suffrage? In the man or in the jackass?

The right to vote has evolved. White men were the primary class of people to become enfranchised in America, being people outside the elite aristocratic class. A chronology of voting rights evolution gives us an historical perspective of the evolution of the right to vote, to include the right of White men to vote. From White male enfranchisement for men without property requirements to the issues of voter qualifications and identity requirements at the polls in 2012, the participation in the electoral process is a participation in the economic decision making of the nation. This researched chronology is as follows:

In 1789, the Establishment of US democracy and the establishment of the principle that White men with property can vote became law. Poor people, Women, Native Americans, and enslaved African-Americans could not vote. From 1770 to 1790, each state has individual naturalization laws. In 1790, Congress passed its first naturalization law to grant citizenship to White men and some women.

The right to vote is tied directly to citizenship status; it is only for Whites who have lived in the country for 2 years. In 1798 the law is changed so immigrant Whites have to live in the US for 14 years before they can become citizens. This changed to 5 years after 1902.

In 1777, women lose the right to vote in New York. That was followed with Massachusetts in 1780 and New Hampshire in 1784. In 1787, the US Constitutional Convention places voting qualifications in the hands of the states. Women in all states except New Jersey lose the right to vote.

State constitutions protecting voting rights for Blacks included those of Delaware (1776), Maryland (1776), New Hampshire (1784), and New York (1777). Pennsylvania also extended such rights in its 1776 Constitution, as did Massachusetts in its 1780 Constitution. As a result of these laws, early American towns like Baltimore had more Blacks than Whites voting in elections. And when the proposed US Constitution was placed before citizens in 1787 and 1788, it was ratified by both Black and White voters in a number of States.

Free Blacks could vote, except in South Carolina, but slaves were not permitted to vote in any State. Under the rule of Great Britain, the abolition of slavery in the Colonies before the Revolution was prohibited. As independent States, they were free to end slavery, which occurred in Pennsylvania, Massachusetts, Connecticut, Rhode Island, Vermont, New Hampshire, and New York. At that time, Blacks in many States not only had the right to vote, but also the right to hold office.

"So, there you have it", I concluded.

"Where do we get the idea that there is a class warfare scenario at work in this election season? It's from the historical divisions of the privileged and the working class that evolved through America's struggle to enfranchise and empower more and more people.

The purpose of the United States is to perpetuate individual freedom, which promotes free enterprise, through free markets, with free people, as entrepreneurs.

The purpose of the United States is to promote the general welfare and secure the blessings of peace for us and our posterity. So, that's how it got started."

America, the Beautiful

In the early years of the Republic, the federal Congress made moves toward ending slavery and thus toward achieving voting rights for all Blacks, not just free Blacks. For example, in 1789 Congress banned slavery in any federally held territory. In 1794, the exportation of slaves from any State was banned; and in 1808, the importation of slaves into any State was also banned.

In 1821, American politics were still largely dominated by deference to the upper classes. Election procedures were, by later standards, quite undemocratic. Most states imposed property and taxpaying requirements on the White adult males who alone had the vote, and they conducted voting by voice. Presidential elections were conducted through State legislations in those days. Given the fact that citizens had only the most indirect say in the election of the President, it is not surprising that voting participation was generally extremely low, amounting to less than 30 percent of adult White males.

Between 1820 and 1840, a revolution took place in American politics. In most states, property qualifications for voting and office holding were repealed and voting by voice was largely eliminated. Direct methods of selecting presidential electors, county officials, state judges, and governors replaced indirect methods. Because of these and other political innovations, voter participation skyrocketed. By 1840 voting participation had reached unprecedented levels. Nearly 80 percent of adult White males went to the polls.

The most significant political innovation of the early nineteenth century was the abolition of property qualifications for voting and officeholding. Hard times resulting from the panic of 1819 led many people to demand an end to property restrictions on voting and officeholding. In New York, for example, fewer than two adult males in five could legally vote for senator or governor. Under the new Constitution adopted in 1821, all adult White males were allowed to vote, so long as they paid taxes or had served in the militia. Five years later, an Amendment to the state's Constitution eliminated the taxpaying and militia qualifications, thereby establishing universal White manhood suffrage. By 1840, universal White manhood suffrage had largely become a reality. Only three states, Louisiana, Rhode Island, and Virginia still restricted the suffrage to White male property owners and taxpayers.

The 1819 application for statehood by the Missouri Territory sparked a bitter debate in Congress over the issue of slavery in the new territories that had been created as a result of the Louisiana Purchase of 1803. Concerned that the South would have a representational advantage, Congressman James Tallmadge of New York introduced an Amendment that would prohibit any further growth of slavery in Missouri, and would eventually set the children of Missouri's slaves free.

Despite "the difficulties and the dangers of having free blacks intermingling with slaves," Tallmadge declared, "I know the will of my constituents, and regardless of consequences, I will avow it; as their representative, I will proclaim their hatred to slavery in every shape." The Bill passed in the House but failed to pass the Senate. The issue was resolved with a two-part compromise. The northern part of Massachusetts became Maine and was admitted to the Union as a free state at the same time that Missouri was admitted as a slave state, thereby maintaining a balance of 12 slave and 12 Free states.

In addition, an imaginary line was drawn at 36 degrees 30 minutes north latitude, above which slavery would not be allowed any portions of the Louisiana Territory lying north of the compromise line. The act also provided that fugitive slaves "escaping into…any state or territory of the United States… may be lawfully reclaimed and conveyed to the person claiming his or her labour or service" -- and even in the free territories, "slavery and involuntary servitude … in the punishment of crimes" was not prohibited. This "fugitive slave" legislation was vehemently opposed by Northerners who felt that they were being compelled to assist in the capture and return of runaways.

In the early 1800's, Northern racism grew directly out of slavery and the ideas used to justify the institution.

The concepts of "black" and "white" did not arrive with the first Europeans and Africans, but grew on American soil. During Andrew Jackson's administration, racist ideas took on new meaning. Jackson brought in the "Age of the Common Man." Under his administration, working class people gained rights they did not have before, particularly the right to vote. But the only people who benefited were White men. Blacks, Indians, and women were excluded.

This was a time when European immigrants were pouring into the North. Many of these people had faced discrimination and hardship in their native countries. But in America they found their rights expanding rapidly. They had entered a country in which they were part of a privileged category called "white."

Classism and ethnic prejudices did exist among White Americans and had a tremendous impact on people's lives. But the bottom line was that for White people in America, no matter how poor or degraded they were, they knew there was a class of people below them.

Poor Whites were considered superior to Blacks and to Indians as well, simply by virtue of being White. Because of this, most identified with the rest of the White race and defended the institution of slavery. Working class Whites did this even though slavery did not benefit them directly and was in many ways against their best interests.

Before 1800, free African American men had nominal rights of citizenship. In some places they could vote, serve on juries, and work in skilled trades. But as the need to justify slavery grew stronger, and racism started solidifying, free Blacks gradually lost the rights that they did have. Through intimidation, changing laws and mob violence, Whites claimed racial supremacy, and increasingly denied Blacks their citizenship. In 1857 the Dred Scott decision, the law formally declared that blacks were not citizens of the United States. From this society, at that time, the White man or the "Common man" was given a system in which to benefit by default, to live with a superior self concept in the slave system, based on color, was the way the world was.

Thus, an identity was born in which privilege over others was granted without any personal sacrifice or requirement except being "white". This gift of status was developed to appease the Common Man in an economy that was growing and adding population, when the Common Man was freed from a European system of indenture and serfdom which was devoid of political participation. For most of the people who comprised the Common Man, his economic power came through the sale of his labor to the factory or the farm. Voting power and knowledge of the economy, in aggregate, was not possible. When the Civil War came, the fight in the Confederacy was to preserve the system and its benefit through an improved (or maintained) status in a New Confederacy.

When the issue was competition for work, for "jobs", the reward was in the re-creation of a system of advantage, following the Civil War. And thereafter, with the Industrialization of America, along came the Labor Movement which was born of the oppression and suppression of the Common Man as Laborer and Proponent of Individual Freedom in the ageless struggle between Capital and Labor, or Power and Numbers.

When the "Union Movement" came, the common economic interest of all working people helped dissolve racial barriers and stereotypes among the Common Man, as labor issues overcame ethnic differences. All of this, of course, transpired under a system of racial segregation before women's suffrage, but it was a beginning of social change. We are all in this struggle, this competition that moves America to greater levels of enfranchisement and participation. For without it, there would be no individual freedom, and without that, no free market system.

The Melting Pot

We live in a melting pot. America is a nation of tribes. There are Blacks and Whites, the people often designated in surveys and census data as the choices we have to make. But we had Whites and Blacks and Indians when the first people populated this country before the Revolutionary War, and pretty much up to the end of the 19th century. And we had Mexicans, but we didn't want to admit it. We also added Europeans such as. Scots and Irish, Germans and Dutch, Swedes and Poles, and Mediterranean people like Italians and Greeks after the Civil War and before that for some. Of course, there were Jews from Russia, all a part of the mass immigration that followed the Civil War and Reconstruction, and the European Wars following the revolts of 1848.

We are a nation of constituencies as well. We have religious people, we have farmers, we have prohibitionist, and we have workers. We have Progressives, we have peace advocates, war advocates, Socialist and Secessionist. We have Peacenics and Militia Movements, and Married people, gay and straight.

All of these groups, urban and rural, compete for their best interests through the lobbying power that we have in this democracy. There are associations of banks, lawyers, manufacturers, and any other trade or professional group that you can imagine. And they may all have overlapping memberships. In this mix, you have to take into consideration the tensions and competitions between ideas, mixed with the prejudices and legal limitations on the minority populations, be they racial or gender based.

All of this flowed through my head when the conversation turned to political differences, like conservatives and liberals and libertarians and populist. What's the difference, really, between someone who is for something or against it if they are not informed. And why should anything else matter?

My thoughts about all this accelerated when Melanie made a comment about voter suppression. She said in a high pitched tone, "And all this stuff about voter ID laws? What do they think is going to happen? If you make people pay, or jump through hoops to vote, you not be able to just limit that to a few people in a few places.

It's like that 80-year-old woman in New Hampshire who has been voting all her life, but had to go out and get a new identification just to be legal at the polls this year. An 80-year-old White woman in New Hampshire is denied the vote because she has to obtain identification to prove who she is when she has proven that for decades without issue. If she didn't have some help in her rural situation, help getting to where she had to go to get all that done, she'd be just as bad off as the people in the cities they're trying to get with these tricks."

This enhanced my thinking about some of the issues that had been on my mind over the course of this election season, issues of political participation and the presence or absence of an economic voice. I kept thinking about Bret and the world that he will grow up to see. He's five years old and he attends a charter school in Washington DC where the student body is one third White, one third Hispanic, and one third Black. This is a new world.

The economy of this country is more diverse than it has ever been. The economy of a country is based upon the people in the country, the culture of the country, and the system of government that oversees commerce and finance.

I say that because, when this country was first founded, it consisted of people from Europe who came to America as a part of the English system of indentured servitude, commonly referred to as the English system. If you didn't own land or have a land grant from the King, you paid your way through indentured servitude or you generally couldn't afford the voyage... generally speaking.

I may mention here that the English system was supplanted by the Spanish system when African slavery was introduced. So we had a melting pot of Europeans and Africans and Native Americans who all shared in the trade that took place within America and between America and the European powers.

Today we have an America which consist of the three cultures above mentioned and the many other immigrants that have come to our shores in the last century and a quarter. This was the beginning of diversity. So we are a melting pot of many Europeans, many Spanish cultures, many African cultures, and many Middle Eastern and Asian cultures, all producing and trading with themselves and the world. This impacts what is produced and what is demanded. But how did we get here?

The American democracy is the framework in which our commerce and finance takes place. The American system of free enterprise provides us with the opportunity to be individually successful due to the protections of the government in our courts and the laws of commerce and finance.

We are free because we live within a governmental system that protects the freedoms of exchange and investment. But as Adam Smith pointed out, Markets can be inefficient if they are systems which restrict free enterprise.

The slavery system, whether it was English or Spanish in nature, it was an inefficient system because it did not allow for wages and prices to find an equilibrium through natural forces.

The history of America has been an evolution to eliminate the barriers to free trade with and between the populations of the country, but this has been a slow process.

After taking a quick sip of lemonade, I continued, giving Melanie my perspective on how we got to be this diverse nation with our global free enterprise society, one that includes worldwide instant telecommunications and people with various degrees of education and understanding, each and every one with a product to sell. We are a part of a globe that has grown into a village. In the world we live in today, we have many economic institutions and organizations that are global, that never existed before 1950.

We have the UN and the IMF of course, and that is complemented by many regional organizations like the European Union. BRIC, and Latin America has one.

The South East Asian nations have one ASEAN), and the Africans have one. The Africans and the Arabs and the Europeans have one together. And the key to all of these groups that oversee the relationships between mankind and nation states is the ability to organize and govern. The problem of how decisions are made has a significant impact on economic activity, be it in the Congress or the European Union or any regulatory body of the government, to include treaty organizations that impact trade activities. The American melting pot is ongoing. Immigration reform seems to be an issue at this time, and I'm sure it will be resolved.

You may say that the impact of immigration began in 1848 with the Treaty of Guadalupe-Hidalgo which ended the Mexican-American War. It also added what was to become one-third of the total territory of the United States.

The treaty guaranteed citizenship to Mexicans living in the newly acquired territories of Arizona, California, New Mexico, Texas and Nevada, but Voting rights were denied. Mexican-Americans who were not allowed to vote despite having US citizenship.

Property laws, language and literacy requirements are used to restrain voting, and Night Riders use intimidation and violence to add to the insult. This was the beginning of this Hispanic cultural inclusion into the American fabric. From that time to this, the census reflects the inclusion of Mexican-Americans into the citizenship of this country.

Black power at the polls and the reflected economic presence began around 1860 when, five states, Maine, New Hampshire, Vermont, Rhode Island and Massachusetts permitted Free Black men to vote (New York allows Free Black men who own at least $250 of property to vote).

In 1866, with the end of the Civil War the year before, the Civil Rights Act of 1866 is passed to grant citizenship to native-born Americans but excludes Native Americans. In 1867, the Fourteenth Amendment passes Congress defining citizen as male, accounting for the first use of the word Male in the Constitution.

As enfranchisement was expanding in America, the rights of White Men to vote were being expanded in England. The English

Parliament passed the Representation of the People Act 1867 (known informally as the Reform Act of 1867 or the Second Reform Act) which was British legislation that enfranchised the urban male working class in England and Wales. Before the Act was passed, only one million of the five million adult males in England and Wales could vote; the act doubled that number, and in its final form, the Reform Act of 1867 enfranchised all male householders. For the African-American, in 1870, the 15th Amendment establishes the right of African-American males to vote. However, poll taxes, reading requirements, physical violence, property destruction, hiding the polls, and economic pressures keep most African-Americans from voting, particularly in this South.

The Ku Klux Klan was a significant contributor to the violence and intimidation used to keep African-Americans from voting. And then, along came the Chinese, builders of the Transcontinental Railroad and descendents of the best gold miners in the 49ers gold rush. No, not the football team, it's not that kind of rushing. It was a gold rush that brought the Chinese to America before the Civil War. They came to dig gold. The Chinese, too, cannot vote.

In 1882, following the construction of the Transcontinental Railroad linking the East Coast of the United States to California, the Chinese Exclusion Act was passed which barred people of Chinese ancestry from becoming citizens. Known also as the Pacific Railroad or the Overland Route, the project was completed in 1869 as one of the major engineering feats of the 19th century. The idea for the railroad to link the two oceans bordering the United States was originally initiated in 1853.

In 1865, with a Silver discovery in Nevada, many of the White workers left the railroad project to join the search for wealth.

As a result, Chinese laborers were hired to replace them, receiving $25 per month in pay as compared to $35 for White men. The Chinese had to buy their own provisions when White men were given room and board.

"So, it seems that this country has taken a lot of history to get to where we are today, awaiting the opportunity to vote and make decisions about our economy.

There are many people in this world who do not have this opportunity, many people who want it. That's one of the reasons people continue to want to come here. We are free and that's what makes for free enterprise", I added.

And we should all be happy about it.

Give Us Your Tired

Immigration has made America. Other than those of Native ancestry, all of us are from somewhere else. But, we are all here now. We make a diversified market and economy, with a global variety of tastes, products, cultures and fashion. But it took us some time to get here. And it took some time to get everybody involved in the decision making about our democracy and our economy, starting with the "first people".

In 1887, The Dawes Act was passed which gives citizenship only to Native Americans who give up their tribal affiliations. In 1890, the Indian Naturalization Act grants citizenship to Native Americans in an application process similar to immigrant naturalization. In 1907, Congress grants citizenship to Native Americans living in Indian Territory, formerly known as Oklahoma.

Prior to 1920, some parts of the United States allowed women to vote, depending upon the issue, and the state. In some cases, for example, women could only vote in school elections. Women in the

Wyoming and Utah territory, and Colorado, have full voting rights prior to 1920. It isn't until 1920 that all women have the right to vote, after the ratification of the 19th amendment to the Constitution.

In 1921, The Sons of America are organized to pursue equality, individual freedom and the rights of Mexican Americans as citizens, including the right to vote. It will be 1975 before the right to vote is available to all Mexican-Americans in the United States.

In 1922, in the case of Takao v. United States, the US Supreme Court upheld the 1790 Naturalization Act that barred Asian-Americans from becoming citizens. This enforces the established policy of denying voting rights for Asian immigrants.

In 1923, in the case of Bhagat Singh Thind v.The US, the court ruled that Asian Indians are eligible for citizenship. Technically, as citizens, they can now vote, in spite of the fact that almost all immigrants who are people of color continue to be denied the right to vote.

In 1924 Native Americans participation in the military during World War I helps to pass the 1924 Indian Citizenship Act. The Act grants Native Americans citizenship, however many western states refuse to allow their enfranchisement. It is well known that some of the tactics used to discourage voting included physical violence, destruction of property, economic pressures, poll taxes, hiding the polls and reading requirements.

In 1943, The Chinese Exclusion Act is repealed, making immigrants of Chinese ancestry eligible for citizenship.

In 1946, Filipinos are allowed to become citizens. In 1952, The McCarran-Walter Act repeals racial restrictions of 1790 Naturalization Law. First generation Japanese can now become citizens.

In 1965, in a direct response to the Civil Rights movement led by Dr. Martin Luther King Jr. and others, The Voting Rights Act of 1965 is enacted, banning literacy tests in the Deep South and providing federal enforcement of Black voter registration and voting rights. This affects the states of Virginia, Alabama, Georgia,

Louisiana, Mississippi, North Carolina, and South Carolina, and also applies in Alaska because of the Eskimos.

The 1970 Voting Rights Act bans literacy tests in 20 states including New York, Illinois, California and Texas. In 1971, the 26th Amendment gives voting rights to 18 year olds in response to protests for men drafted for the Vietnam War under the age of 21.

In 1975, The Voting Rights Act is amended to include language assistance to minority voters. Language requirements have been used routinely to keep the vote from US born citizens who speak other languages.

In 1990, The Americans with Disabilities Act requires access to the polls and to the ballot. In 2000, with the Vote fraud scandals in Florida and elsewhere, thousands of eligible voters are prevented from voting and at least one million ballots are never counted.

In the campaign of 2012, many states enacted laws that challenged voter identity, as our 80 year-old voter demonstrated earlier.

Many of these laws have been struck down by the courts and some have suggested that these challenges have organized and motivated the very people they are designed to disenfranchise. It is clear to me that the statement made by Thomas Jefferson, which is written on the back of his Monument in Washington, DC is as current as it was when he said it, "Eternal vigilance is the price of freedom".

The United States population is diverse and continues to move in that direction. New immigrants have been arriving since the beginning of the nation and will continue until the end of it or of time.

The country's population, according to government and private research estimates, will grow from 282.1 million in 2000 to 419.9 million in 2050. This 49% population increase will be in contrast to most European countries whose populations are expected to decline over the same period. The decline in US population will consist primarily of non-Hispanic whites which will decrease from its current 69.4% to 50.1% of the population by 2050.

The largest population increase will be in the Hispanic population, with a projected increase from 35.6 million in 2002 2102.6 million in 2050. The Hispanic portion of the population will increase over that time, from 12.6% to 24.4%.

The Black population is projected to increase from 35.8 million in 2000 261.4 million in 2050, an increase of approximately 26,000,000 people. The proportion of African American people in the US population would rise from 12.7% to 14.6%.

The Asian population is projected to grow from10.7 million in 2000 to 33.4 million in 2050. The countries Asian population is projected to increase from 3.8% to 8% during this period. The country's population is also projected to become older over the coming years, with about one in five people being over 65 by the year 2030.

The current trend of immigration patterns continues to consist of the diverse population from all over the world as new American immigrants.

However, people of Hispanic origin will become the largest proportion of that minority, in a nation where the majority of the people will not be able to trace their ancestry back to Europe. In 1990, Mexican immigration accounted for about 22% of all immigrants coming to America. By 2000, this number had grown to about 30% of the total number of immigrants coming to America.

Research indicates that immigration from all of Latin America, immigrants from Spanish-speaking countries, increased from 37% to 46% of the total foreign-born population during the 1990s, with more than 60% of the growth in foreign-born population coming from Spanish speaking immigrants.
States in the South West, like Arizona and Texas, have seen the greatest impact of this immigration.

This is an immigration that is changing the political dimensions of this nation, adding diversity to the decision-making process and our republican democracy, and changing commercial and cultural buying patterns.

And although this population was significantly Republican for a greater part of the 20th century, recent elections have demonstrated a Democratic Party lien by these new voters.

The impact of this trend will change the nature of the economic concerns of the American people and the resulting public policy. The question is, what will be the impact of these new voters and buyers on the American economy and its politics?

With this new demographic, new questions arise and new inquiries about the impact of political change on economic are being made by those who evaluate the economy.

If the landless White Male in America could see how he has been in the pocket of the wealthy landowner, to the wealthy industrialist, to the wealthy politician, without gaining anything other than an identity that holds itself together with the barometer of another people, he would abandon the social conservative values that were given to him and embrace a new world order of live and let live.

In doing that, he would appreciate the fact that unions represent his participation in alleviating the burdens of the free enterprise system that reward capital and challenges the cost and freedom of labor. He would remember the history of his own enfranchisement and would not forget the lessons of Blair Mountain in West Virginia and the times when his labor was considered to be as cheap as a slave.

The Common Man, in this instance, is the cultural demographic of rural and agrarian people who have a history that mingles their identity with the benefit of privilege within the American historical evolution. He will remember that his destiny is not tied to the progress or failure of another and he would likely learn from that emergence that his vote should be in his own interest, and not that of conservative causes that may be blinded by the links politicians may make to that identity when it serves their best interest. When that bias enters the discussion, consciously or not, it keeps him in the back pockets of such politicians who come with promises of wealth, acceptance and participation that never are realized.

It's a false notion to think that the nation you live in can be better if the leader fails. That logic can only be supported by emotions that are hard to identify and difficult to touch, unless you know who you are. Today, we are all in this thing together. The fight to be free and competitive, organized and unified, and ready for the 21st century global competition, is in everyone's interest.

"You don't have to take my word for it" as I reached for a book on the table next to me, holding it up as a sign, " Read Huckleberry Finn by Mark Twain, in its original version, and listen to what he is saying about that", I spoke as I waved a book around for everyone to see. Bret wasn't moved by any of it.

Measuring the Money

I took a breath and I asked myself, "What will the world be like for my five-year-old nephew when he grows to manhood? What will work in those times and what will be important when that time arrives?"

I spoke out loud to Melanie, "Deuteronomy! What have we learned? And then I began a recap.

First off, we learned that Economics is the allocation of scare resources among alternative uses, based on supply (resources) and demand (uses). We know that supply and demand determine price. We learned that the government decides what kind of economic system will exist and how much freedom it will contain. We learned that land, labor and capital, (and information) are the tools of the Entrepreneurs and we learned that everybody does not have an equal say in the economic system because, historically, everybody does not have the same money, power or status (rights) in the society.

We live in a diverse society and a diverse world. It took a few millenniums to get here, but we are all here now. We are connected by a global network of communications and transportation that makes the globe a village and we trade with each other in the exchange of scare resources, in the process of maintaining peace on this flying platform of 6,000,000,000 souls. We are on board the Spaceship Enterprise from Star Trek, and we are learning to work and play together.

In the new world order, people will be living in a more democratic world, one where land, labor and capital will be important, and the rules of economics will be basically the same. The only things that will change will be the need and importance of information. Information technology has opened the opportunity to create a global economic community that resolves global problems by creating organized efforts that can be effectively managed, and to communicate information from those who have expertise to those who don't. It's a division of labor with thinking as a competitive advantage.

With the new world order, we will face the issues of climate, the ecology, trading systems, and the extraction of resources as challenges at a higher level.

As we learned, Economics is the allocation of resources, among alternative uses, in most cases scarce resources, and the manipulation of land labor capital and entrepreneurship to achieve economic goals. Whether these goals are for the coffers of the King or to promote the general welfare, that is the objective of an economic system. And to be sure we are moving in the right direction, we need to have information about the economy and its impacts. Econometrics is the merging of statistics, mathematics and economics for the purpose of giving us a clearer empirical understanding of the economy and its direction. This field of study was developed in the early part of the 1900s to provide clarity to analysis of economic activity. We also need to understand the difference between macroeconomics and microeconomics, when we are doing analysis of the economy.

Macroeconomics is this study of our economy as a whole and the relationships between the components of the whole. Microeconomics consists of the study of the components of the economy at the smallest level, businesses and individuals, and the impact upon these components of economic activity. As a part of achieving this goal, the United States government created the Bureau of Labor Statistics.

The Bureau of Labor was established in the Department of the Interior by the Bureau of Labor Act (23 Stat. 60), June 27, 1884, to collect information about employment and labor. It became an independent (sub-Cabinet) department by the Department of Labor Act (25 Stat. 182), June 13, 1888. It was incorporated, as the Bureau of Labor, into the Department of Commerce and Labor by the Department of Commerce Act (32 Stat. 827), February 14, 1903. Finally, it was transferred to the Department of Labor in 1913 where it resides today.

The Bureau of Labor Statistics (BLS) is a unit of the United States Department of Labor. It is the principal fact-finding agency for the U.S. government in the broad field **of** labor economics and statistics. The BLS is a governmental statistical agency that collects, processes, analyses, and disseminates essential statistical data to the American public, the U.S. Congress, other Federal agencies, State and local governments, business, and labor representatives. The BLS also serves as a statistical resource to the Department of Labor and reports periodically on the unemployment rate among other notable statistics.

The BLS data must satisfy a number of criteria, including relevance to current social and economic issues, timeliness in reflecting today's rapidly changing economic conditions, accuracy and consistently high statistical quality, and impartiality in both subject matter and presentation. To avoid the appearance of partiality, the dates of major data releases are scheduled more than a year in advance, in coordination with the Office of Management and Budget. You also find that a lot of government information has a scheduled release under confidentiality laws to protect time sensitive information. In the past, any such information took snail mail to get it. Now, you can go to USA.gov and get all the business data and statistics you can imagine, and all for free.

With the end of the age of conflicts, with this New World Order in which dictators are rejected for the freedom and participation of democracy, peace leads to prosperity which leads to consumption. This has always been the case, following the great wars and other smaller continuous conflicts. Consumption is the driving force of the economy. Consumer demand must be measured in order to effectively intervene and solve economic problems through monetary and fiscal policies.

When inflation rises, we want to cut the supply of money. When the economy cools down, we want to inject money into the economy through government policies. We want to measure the employment rate and the rate of consumption for an understanding where we are and where we're going.

This information is the basis for economic policymaking. Choosing the right information will depend upon the questions asked and the measurements required, for measuring the economy is imperative to managing its movement.

So, these things, these issues of information, will comprise the economy of the future. These things, and many other things, that previously had no impact on the economy will be important in making economic decisions, be they microeconomics or macroeconomic. As we learned, economics happens within the framework of government. It doesn't matter if there's a tribe, a kingdom or a democracy, the enterprise between human beings is promoted or regulated by the state. The government sets the framework for economic activity.

That's true in the New World, just like in the old one, that idea of limits and order. Human beings like order. They like to know what time the bank opens and how to calculate their taxes.

In the New World, they'll be doing this over the Internet or through some other satellite connected electromagnetic telecommunications system that links individuals, one to another, or in groups. And that New World will have to consider some aspects of the elements of economics that we had not considered before. One example is rare earth elements.

Rare earth elements are valuable to the new economy because they are the scarce resources that make computers run and cell phones work. The rare earth minerals consist of a group of 17 chemical elements. If you use a computer, a DVD, rechargeable batteries, cell phones, car catalytic converters, magnets, or fluorescent lighting, you used rare earth element or strategic metals as they are sometimes called.

So, is it that we should concern ourselves with rare earth elements and strategic minerals because they are considered to be something that would be needed to supply the military and industry?

Should we be concerned that they are essential to the needs of the economy in which we flourish, to the extent that they may impact on our ability to respond in an emergency situation? The geopolitical balance, in every way, is impacted by these new minerals. The global mineral supply is primarily available in the countries of the former Soviet Union, China and South Africa. They are strategic minerals because they are needed by the Western world to operate the high tech military equipment that makes our country safe. So that's the new economics which will eventually have an impact on the price of a sandwich in Baltimore.

Rare Earth elements and metals will be as important to the economies of developed nations as oil is today. Once again, it's important to remember that peace and prosperity go hand-in-hand. With peace comes consumption, and with consumption comes economic activity that is supported by demand. Demand creates supply, or finds the right price to make it worthwhile for everyone involved to be paid, and this creates jobs.

But none of this will happen if there is no peace. The struggle for scarce resources has been the cause of many wars, so it is important to keep in mind that it is better to cooperate than to have a conflict which destroys peace and reduces consumption. Because, war is not good for children and other living things, and peace is good for everybody.

As a framework for planning and building an economic future, we need to consider that there are many issues that will impact economics that have not impacted economics in the past. Oh yes, the issues of demand will be the same, people will need food, water, shelter and clothing. People will need to express themselves and want to feel empowered. People will have the potential to solve any problem that people can create, just like now. In tomorrow's world, people will think of the economy from a global perspective. Any entertainment of economics without an understanding of the global influences is not taking a strategic and broad view of the future.

The Classical approach to Economics operates under the premise that the economy always gets better on its own.

Left alone, business cycles always go back and correct themselves. No government interference was needed, they believed.

In 1919, John Maynard Keynes argued for a greater role by government in financing the development of a nation or correcting the results of an economic crisis. In the book titled, "The Economic Consequences of the Peace", John Maynard Keynes argued that the Versailles Treaty was too harsh and austere to Germany, arguing that a negative response would evolve from this austere plan and that, to the contrary, the injection of funds for economic growth would have been a better approach.

When that predicted catastrophe came in the form of Adolph Hitler, who came to power 14 years later, people began to appreciate Keynes policy as an approach to nation building.
It is interesting that today Germany is making similar austerity demands on Greece, encouraging them to cut their budget as a way of solving the global economic crisis, or at least the part that the European Union is dealing with today.

Keynes suggested that an economic slump can be rescued by spending money the government does not have to stimulate economic activity that will build an economy that will create taxes to pay for the cost of growth. The Marshall Plan, following World War II, is an example of what Keynes had in mind in his book. With a stimulus package or stimulus spending, the government provides money in place of private capital to cut interest rates and to enhance borrowing and increase business activity. Extra spending will pay for itself, at the bottom of the business cycles, even if the government needs to borrow from the Banks. By the way, most of the current $16 Trillion debt of the United States is held by US citizens and institutions who have invested in government bonds, not China, Japan or the Gulf State Nations..

The philosophy of John Maynard Keynes can be seen through the New Deal of President Roosevelt in the construction of Hoover Dam and its multiplier effect, where many more jobs and economic infrastructure followed Hoover Dam than just its singular economic benefit.

A similar impact will occur with the construction of an urban Metro Station or a rural truck stop, or a major sports complex.

Faced with a Great Depression, when individuals and businesses stopped spending money, the government must spend. This was characterized by John Maynard Keynes as activist government. But now, the debt level is as never before.

One of the contributions of economists like John Maynard Keynes is the idea of measuring the economy. Economics (from the Greek for oikos meaning household and nomikos meaning usage, custom, laws) means the measurement of the ecosystem, us and our eco-activity. Economists began to measure the economy by asking people questions and measuring the relationships between economic enterprises.

In today's world, all economic activity must consider the relationships it has to the entire global marketing system. This allows for a clearer picture because there are no boundaries, no frontiers and no empires that are outside of a relationship with world. As was once written in song, "We are the world".

In the new world economy, we have the same components as with the Classical model. The issues will be how we use what we have and how we allocate these resources throughout the globe, or within our own economy. Land is still my land, no matter how you measure it. It consist of all that can be produced from it, to include minerals, commodities, energy, food, wood, metals, water and critical materials, all aspects of land as an element to be measured for economic management.

When measuring the elements of land, you should consider that critical materials like rare earth elements are important because of their new influences in technology.

The land gives us a variety of commodities, to include water. Let us not forget water because technology may help us avert water issues that previously would have been a problem. But there is a demand for water now that previously did not exist. In the Western United States, in the Middle East, and in various parts of Latin America, Asia and Africa, there are water problems.

Of all of the water on Earth, 97% is salient and 2% is in icecaps and glaciers. Water also cost money. 99 gallons of water per day is used by the average American. It's 1,500 gallons if you include industrial use.

The labor environment is in transition worldwide. Immigration, or migration from developing countries to develop countries, is a reason for some economic turmoil, as worker competition, the demand for low-wage employees and the cost of immigrant population growth are all concerns in the modern world for developed nations.

These economic impacts have forced Europe to make decisions about its future, about its sovereign debt, the euro as a currency, Europe as a state regulator, and the role of the European Union. Decisions about the banking systems in global finance, and the relationships of those entities between Europe, its previous colonial nations in Africa and Asia, and the United States are currently under discussion.

Global governance has an impact on all of these issues as it impacts how we make these agreements between ourselves as a nation and as a body of nations.

Global governance is an emerging concept, and you can't govern without proper information. The United Nations followed the League of Nations, and subsequent to that, the world has created many regional trade and cooperation organizations in Africa, Asia, the Caribbean and Latin America. The European Union is a good example.

These international systems of governance in the management and oversight of the global economy have expanded to the establishment of the GATT (the Global Agreement on Tariffs and Trade), the World Bank and the International Monetary Fund, and the World Trade Organization. These institutions, like so many around the world, regulate trade through treaties and regional agreements that have been established over time.

As time passes into the future, this governance will be impacted and reestablished as new commodities and relationships with new nations and new labor issues as changes in the global community take place. We have to understand the global economic world we live in. If we're going to manage it, we need to measure it.

I turned to Bret, pointing and saying, "Bret, that toy you have probably wouldn't work without rare earth elements either, so keep that in mind."

The New World Order

Bret gently put his toy on the floor and looked at me, wide-eyed and said," So what's it going to be like?" Melanie and I glanced at each other and exchanged the feeling that he might be listening with intention.

"Go 'head"! Melanie suggested. So I told him.

The earth is undergoing a change. In that change, we are discovering that there is a global water crisis that threatens the stability of nations and the health of billions. This is due to the fact that the issues of water are issues that are issues of technology, ecology and politics.

In the year 2009, NASA satellites measured changes in the mass of underground water in northern India, yielding data that confirmed excessive irrigation practices were sucking the water from the aquifer.

The fact that the population grew to the point that has drained the aquifer, draining groundwater levels, by as much as a foot per year, is shocking. This could impact 114 million residents of the region if agriculture collapsed and potable water was to evaporate, according to sources.

The aquifers or groundwater used on Earth are historically drawn from depths of 20 to 30 feet below the surface, and was plentiful throughout our history. When fossil fuel became the norm, this allowed us to pump water from deeper depths. Since then, we have lived beyond the ability of the supply of water to renew itself. Icecaps are melting and sources of rivers are not being replenished to the degree they were in the past, impacting on water supplies worldwide.

According to the UN, groundwater extraction has tripled globally in the last 50 years. This was a timeframe in which India and China use groundwater 10 times greater than they had before. The result is that half of the global population lives in nations where water tables are rapidly declining.

The problem is enhanced by new patterns in land use, like forced irrigation and soil grading, as well as leakage from poorly maintained infrastructure in cities. Yeah! People are not perfect with the resources that we have. There is always a broken water pipe somewhere.

The need for the management of water is driving some Economists think in terms of applying a value to the commodity so that we can better manage it. Scarcity is one of the tenants of economics, the distribution of scarce resources among alternative uses. The issue is enhanced by bad water management, including the over pumping of groundwater supplies, wasteful irrigation practices, deforestation, and soil grading, according to the National Intelligence Council. With that said, the OECD has predicted that, by 2030, nearly half of the world's population will be living under severe water stress. But we'll get through this too.

And then there is the issue of capital. You can't have an economy without capital. And where is the capital? Well, is in the banks.

When asked, John Dillinger, a famous gangster in the 1930s once said that he robbed banks because that's where the money was. The global system of financing cannot happen without the banks acting as both creators of capital and as regulators of currency.

In the past, Markets were controlled by the King through land grants, Charters and Appointments. And the King was in charge. He had ownership of everything, from the land to the Peasant on the land, to the gold collected through trade among nations or from wars. Business was conducted in exchange for gold and any other tribute or thing of value. The King's treasure, which was collected in taxes and wars, was the method of government finance from the time of the Egyptian empire to the King of England in 1776.

Around that time, the world was coming out of the Mercantile period. The New World Encyclopaedia defines that period as follows:

"Mercantilism is an economic system that dominated the major European trading nations during the sixteenth, seventeenth, and eighteenth centuries. This "mercantile system" was based on the premise that national wealth and power were best served by increasing exports and collecting precious metals in return. It superseded the medieval feudal organization in Western Europe, especially in the Netherlands, France, and England. Domestically, this led to some of the first instances of significant government intervention and control over the economy, and it was during this period that much of the modern capitalist system was established. Internationally, mercantilism encouraged the many European wars of the period and fuelled European imperialism."

Mercantilism was finally challenged by advocates of "laissez-faire", such as Adam Smith in "The Wealth of Nations", who argued that international and domestic trade were both important, and that it was not the case that one country must grow wealthy at the expense of another. As this and other economic ideas arose throughout the nineteenth century, the mercantilist view was superseded.

Nonetheless, many of the ideas and policies have not been forgotten, emerging again as circumstances changed. For example, the Great Depression of the early twentieth century created doubts about the efficacy and stability of free market economies, providing a new role for governments in the control of economic affairs. John Maynard Keyes was one of those advocates.

When Silver became plentiful, after the voyages of Columbus to America, it spawned the time of the Pirate, like the ones in the "Pirates of the Caribbean" movies. It was a time in which Piracy became the norm in the Atlantic Ocean, a time in which Kings followed a policy of commissioning privatized military ships to help represent their economic interest in the competition among the nations of Europe. This was a period when Silver became available in consistent amounts large enough to melt, measure and weigh.

After the discovery of these large Silver deposits in the Americas, Silver became a medium of exchange, a currency that people could use in trade or in the exchange for goods or commodities, and would be accepted at a fixed or determinable (or agreeable) rate of exchange. This allowed for the expansion of the global trading system through the exchange of Silver coins called "Pieces of Eight". Trade expanded, markets grew and the economic level of Europe's people was improved.

Silver allowed for the expansion of the global trade and commerce through the establishment of new networks among different nations. That led to the modern world by providing a stable currency for the banking sector to use in financing the slave trade, the cotton trade, the sugar trade, the tobacco trade, the coffee trade, the tea trade, the fur trade, the rum trade and the funds needed to build Chartered colonies and new states in the New World.

Now the banking system is simple. From its inception, in Holland in the modern era, banks collected currency from various sources. These sources included individuals, governments, The Catholic Church or organized trade groups, providing banks with the money to make loans to finance trade. With a common currency, it was easy to conduct business. Language was not a barrier, not with a Silver coin.

So the banks collected money and made loans. And when the loan was repaid, the profits from the loan allowed the bank to make money. It also allowed for a return of some of the profit to the depositors of funds. Many ordinary people got rich in that period.

All of this required Collateral. Collateral is the asset or valuable property that the bank holds in order to guarantee that the bank will not lose money, and that the depositors will not lose money, unless all the loans go bad. Banks also charge fees for various transactions, some of which remain with banks to this day and some of which have been usurped from their authority by government. So that's the way it works. That's the way it worked then and that's the way it works now. It's very simple, but banks are not the only player in the financial system.

Today banks are regulated by governments. The recent financial crisis that we have just experienced is the result of many economic influences, but the banks are always key because they are the institutions that the government uses to regulate the financial system.

The reason the banks are regulated is because of the many "Bank Crisis" experienced by the public and the investor community during our history. They are regulated in the United States by the Treasury Department and the Federal Reserve System.

Banks in Europe are not as regulated as those in the United States, but now, with the European Banking Crisis, the European Union is beginning to oversee much more of what goes on there. Banks all over the world are regulated at different levels by their governments. There are international agreements that regulate the transfer of funds and currencies between banks around the world, regulating exchanges and currency values

There are other financial players that are less regulated by the government, like Wall Street investment firms and hedge funds. But it appears the government is working to change that. Recent regulations and proposed legislation is intended to address some of the concerns that America felt following our 2008 Recession, with its Real Estate Crash, Housing Bubble, Mortgage Foreclosure Crisis, Jobs Crisis, Government Bailout and the Banking Crisis that lead to the Bailout.

People are now asking the government for answers to an uncontrolled financial system that operates outside of the banking system.

There is a law called Dodd-Frank that will have historical implications on how this all moves along. But that's for another discussion.

What's The Way Out?

As the sun began to set in the west, flowing streams of bright yellow and golden light creased its way through the trees surrounding the porch, creating the impression of a series of spot lights on the lawn and scrubs. I took a sip of tea, draining the bottom of the cup with a loud slurp. Bret turned and looked at me as if I had done the most horrendous and embarrassing thing and gave me a frown with his hands on the nose.

"That was rude?!", he hummed.

I returned his comment with a strong, closed mouth smile and said, "But it was good!"

Melanie commented, "But not a good role model". Melanie Added, "It's getting late and we are going to have to go soon". Bret frowned again. Melanie turned to me and asked, "So, how do we get out of this mess?"

I took a second to form an idea that Bret might get something out of and I went on to talk about the economic climate we're living in and what it all seems to be saying to us. Saying things like "wake up" and "get busy". With the setting sun, we rose and gathered our things, while sauntering towards the house, and I continued the conversation.

I've heard the idea that we must give Job Creators all the leeway and tax cuts they need so that they can create the jobs in the economy, suggesting that the job losses we've experienced in the last few years was the result of regulations and tax increases that happened in recently. Yet, we have had periods in our history with higher taxes and more regulations and we were fine then.

The idea that Job Creators, the wealthy individuals, large corporations and financial institutions, or enterprises that comprise what can be described as the "Economic Elite" of a nation, are the sole source of jobs is to suggest that the jobs we have would not exist without them.

The idea also makes no allowance for the economy we live in and the types of jobs in it. Just like the physical infrastructure of bridges, roads, communications lines, utilities and transportation systems, the Economic Elite is that segment of the private sector or commercial economy that provides the bulk or Leading Sector industries and enterprise that move the economy.

But they are not alone. Small business, cottage enterprise, black markets and transfer payments comprise a significant and necessary portion of the economy, if not most of it. Remember, we didn't have jobs before the Industrial Revolution, we had an agrarian economy. Now, it's a service economy and you don't need a factory to provide a service like shoe shines or income tax returns.

It's a nation's competitive advantage, you might say. Adam Smith might call it an oligarchy. In some instances, you could define it as "the monopoly of the aristocracy".

If you'll recall, all the wealth in America belonged to the King of England and he doled it out to whom he pleased, friends and family. Those people became the "job creators" because they were endowed with the opportunity to control commerce. It was not a Democracy, but it was still an economy.

As such Leading Sector players, being too big to fail, the Leading Sector industries and producers, whether they be shipbuilders, traders, slavers, whalers, plantation owners, manufacturers or financiers, hold a pivotal position in the economy. No matter the country, whether it's the oligarchy of steel and cars in Japan, cocoa and coffee in Kenya, Gold and diamonds in South Africa, or financing and currency exchange in Switzerland, the Leading Sectors are the Economic Elite of that country.

Economic activity created by government, to some extent, provides stability and control over these markets and allows for "Laissey Faire", the freedom to pay yourself without interference from King or another Commoner.

It's the idea of being a Free Mason is applied to commerce, which evolved out of the desire to be free to sell one's labor. That is the definition of a freeman. Jobs are created by free men and women in free trade and commerce. When they get rich, they will stop creating jobs and start giving money to charity, which is good. But, that's just my take on it.

As we entered the house, Melanie turned to catch a glimpse of the calm in the evening. It was quiet, and the sky was filled with jet engine entrails crossing a buttermilk sky. And we could see the shades turning into shadows as we moved indoors. The TV was on now and lights in the living room shared their glow with us as we left the porch while sounds of political discussions could be heard coming from the TV.

Bret looked up at me with his big dark eyes as if he was about to ask me a question. I wondered to myself if it were a "why" question. Kids always ask the question "why?"

But this time, it wasn't. Bret asked me, with his arms and hands spread out to each side, with a toy car pointed to the ceiling. "Well, what's the way out?"

We found our way inside and sat down, making ourselves comfortable on the sofa in the living room as smells of a hot chili gravitated from the kitchen into our senses. I sat back and thought to myself for a second, and thinking to myself, "How do I answer that question? I gave it my best.

I tried to relate to Bret, as a five-year-old kid, as best I could and gave him my thoughts.

"Now, let me tell you a story about the Wizard of Oz. I'm going to tell you a few fairy tales, like before, when you were two, but I'm going to add a little real world stuff to it while I tell it. It's a story of Adam Smith, the Neo-Classicals, the Keynesians and the Monetarists on his way down the yellow brick road to see the Wizard of Oz. This was long after Dorothy and Toto left, many many years.

This Wizard is like many of the other Wizards that stands behind the curtain and manipulates the strings. But in the end, when the curtain is removed, they tell you the truth. Paul Volcker is one of those Wizards.

And I'm going to end the story with a visit to the Wizard of Oz in his seat in front of the curtain, in front of the British Parliament to address some questions about the relationships between banks in the United States and in the United Kingdom, following calls for a better set of rules for banks. I don't want us to start off lost, so let me slow down and just say a little about how we got from the Gold Standard to where we are now.

I was fortunate enough to catch a portion of the testimony Paul Volcher gave while watching the event on C-SPAN on October 17, 2012, when Volcker was ending his testimony before this committee of the British Parliament. This is an example of the new world we live in. You can get information about the economy while drinking tea at home.

In Volcher's testimony, he made it clear that the problems in Europe and the United States was the problem of people coming to an agreement as to what should be done and taking the steps to allow it to happen. Politics is the problem with the economy.

Again, governments have to make it work. Paul Volcker was an American economist. He was the Chairman of the Federal Reserve under United States Presidents Jimmy Carter and Ronald Reagan. He is widely credited with ending the high levels of inflation seen in the United States in the 1970s and early 1980s. He was the Chairman of the Economic Recovery Advisory Board under President Barack Obama from February 2009 until January 2011. In many ways you may say that he is the embodiment of the Wizard of Oz.

Paul Volker represents the Wizard who is able to see the economy from behind the curtain or vale of financial secrecy, about how things work and who gets what.

As we know by now, the way to get out of the economic mess that we're in is not by allowing banks to become too big or mortgages to become too unregulated, or government to become too lazy or corrupt. Nothing changes until the people decide to change it. When the people can work together to understand, they can work together to petition for solutions. But they must know what they are talking about, or at least what their politicians are talking about.

In this democracy, the people are the power. Whether it's a struggle with the King of England or strife with a robber baron, the people need not turn against the government, the people need to become more OF the government.

In the early 1900s, Teddy Roosevelt fought the robber barons to keep Trusts, conglomerates, cartels, the elite, the aristocracy, the landowners and the oligarchy from taking this country from the hands of the people to the board rooms of corporations. Teddy Roosevelt was a Trust Buster.

In the 1930s, Franklin Roosevelt instituted legislation that led to the development of the middle class from the society of the Common Man, people who previously did not have the education and housing opportunities that emerged from Farmer's Home Administration and the Federal Housing Administration or the G.I. Bill, or the energy from the Tennessee Valley Authority to build a better life in rural America.

The support of the government during the Civil Rights Movement enfranchised a segment of America and prepared a generation for service and economic contributions, freely and unfettered. As Adam Smith says, a free society where everyone can sell their labor is the most productive society.

This may be a good time to talk about immigrants, illegal immigrants, or any other kind of immigrants to the United States. According to what I've heard, there are many misconceptions about immigrants and their contribution or drain on the American economy.

The national Academy of sciences did a study that calculated the taxes of US immigrants and their descendents at a positive $80,000 over their lifetimes after subtracting the cost of government services they're likely to use.

Likewise, the urban Institute calculated that all immigrants arriving in the United States between 1970 and 1992 paid taxes that outstrip their costs for welfare and other social services during this period by $25-$30 billion. In either case, studies indicate that immigration does not have a significant effect on overall US employment. The explanation is that new entrants not only fill jobs, they also create jobs through their purchasing power and by starting new businesses. There is indication through studies that States with relatively small immigrant populations had higher unemployment rates than those with a large immigrant presence. Who'd a thunk it?

So now our problem is that we have had banks that are too big to fail. We have had nations (like Greece) that are too big to fail and we have had businesses, like Enron and Arthur Anderson that were too big to fail.

And why did these enterprises fail? They failed because there was a lack of oversight by responsible people, particularly government, and misinformation about assets and collateral that the banks depended upon for reserves. Of course there were many other reasons for the big bank failures and economic crisis in real estate in America, and the subsequent exportation of undervalued real estate and mortgage assets to the world, but, the decisions of government, or the lack thereof, is the major reason.

Government oversight changes the confidence in the economy by providing the guarantee that someone is looking, and that that someone is responsible and concerned about maintaining a positive economy. But there's also greed and mismanagement that adds to the problem. And all these things are done by people.

So when the people have an understanding of the economy and how it works and what it does, and they apply that knowledge to their lives and to their politics, the chances of anything becoming too big to fail or to fail because of a lack of oversight will be minimized. Knowledge is power.

In an exclusive interview with The Daily Telegraph, according to Senior City Correspondent, Helia Ebrahimi who reported on this story on 23 Sep 2012, Mr. Volcker said that plans to force banks in the UK to ring-fence their traditional retail arms from "casino" investment divisions would not work in the event of a bail out. This was in response questions about big banks, those that are considered "too big to fail". The idea of separating retail operations from commercial banking, or hedge funds from account holding functions, is called Ringfencing. Ringfencing, he said, would only work in "fair-weather" conditions, but not when banks were under pressure.

"In my experience ring-fencing is not terribly effective," said Mr. Volcker. "It only works in fair-weather. But doesn't work in foul weather. They have already run into problems and they are bound to run into more."

As reported, Mr. Volcker hit out against the political grid lock and the billions spent in lobbying in Washington, which he says risks corrupting the political system ahead of the upcoming US elections.

"I am really disturbed about the power of money in Washington. By the end of this election more than $1bn will have been spent by each candidate. We are in danger of getting to a place where the US government risks being for sale. That is a valid concern."

The sunset was beautifully that evening. You could see the oranges and the reds and those shades of gray that accompany a beautiful sunset, with streams of light melting into a bluer and darker sky. I think Bret slept well that night, but we will see what world he wakes up to in the morning.

But what we know for sure is that the new world he lives in will be a democratic, globally- linked and connected marketplace where each and every man has a product to sell, transforming himself into the currency that is needed somewhere in the world. Through the Internet, that democracy will evolve over time with the coming fall of autocratic systems and the ability to communicate with anyone and everyone all the time.

 That economic construct will continue as long as people understand how the economy works and that the key ingredient is knowledge. I want Bret to remember that there were no "jobs" before 1840 when the "Industrial Revolution" began in England. We lived in an agrarian world, everywhere in the world. The Industrial Revolution evolved into the Service economy, the economy in which we live today.

In the US, "Since the conclusion of World War II, at which time service industries accounted for 10% of nonfarm employment, compared with 38% for manufacturing, things have changed. Since the 1970s the American economy has moved away from producing goods to providing services, and the service-producing sector has accounted for an increasing proportion of workers. In 1970, for example, there were 48.8 million service-providing workers, and 22.2 million people in the goods-producing sector, representing a service-to-goods ratio of 2.2 to one.

By 2000, the number of workers in the service-providing sector was 107.1 million, compared with 24.6 million in the goods-producing sector, representing a service-to-goods ratio of 4.4 to one.

In 2005, according to preliminary statistics compiled by the Bureau of Labor Statistics and published in *Establishment Data Historical Employment* (2005), workers who provided services (111.5 million) outnumbered workers who produced goods (22.1 million) by a ratio of five to one." (This is sourced from The American Workplace - The Shift To A Service Economy - Jobs, Million, Industry, and Workers – StateUniversity.com)

I want Brett to know that he will be living in a globally-connected, culturally diverse, energy competitive, water rationing, rare earth demanding, electronic funds transferring, politically democratic planet with environmental, health and food issues, Free Enterprise involves responsibility and Capitalism involves risk. I want him to know that knowledge of the economic system is both good for him and good for his ability to work with it. For as the Bible says: "A Feast is made for laughter, and wine maketh merry: but money answereth all things"-Ecclesiastes 10:19

About the Author

Carrington B. Davis is a native Washingtonian who has degrees in Economics, Business and Public Administration from Howard, Wharton and the University of Southern California. He served as an Engineer Officer during the Viet Nam War before his tenure as President of the Anacostia Economic Development Corporation in Washington, DC. His experience includes economic development, management and policy, from small business to commercial and infrastructure real estate development with varied institutions such as the US Department of the Interior, the US small Business Administration, the Tennessee Valley Authority and the Atlanta Underground Festival Project. He worked as a Budget Examiner in the Management Services Division of the Office of the President, Office of Management and Budget, and with the US Price Commission in 1972.His first real world experience came as a Management Consultant with KPMG in Washington, DC. He was Executive Director of the National Dental Association and a member of the faculty at Howard University School of Business and Public Administration in Washington, DC, and is currently CEO of Philanthropic Cultural Expressions, Inc. in Washington, DC.